Environmental regulation of tourism

Strategies and prospects on three European islands:
Bornholm, Mallorca and the Isle of Wight

by

Anne-Mette Hjalager

Unit of Tourism Research
at
Research Centre of Bornholm
in
co-operation with
Advance/1 (Anne-Mette Hjalager)

November 1996

Preface

In 1994 the Research Centre of Bornholm was established and has since carried out tourism research as a major field of research. The centre has launched into a number of studies comprising for instance the nature of special interst tourism, economic modelling of tourism expenditures and local economic impacts, labour market and educational issues of tourism and service quality development.

Part of the research finds its empirical base on the island of Bornholm, an appropriate place for case studies, as tourism accounts for a substantial proportion of the economic activity. Also in this book it can be observed that Bornholm is in focus.

It is the ambition of the Reserach Centre of Bornholm to participate in the ongoing international co-operation in tourism research. This publication is an excellent exponent for this ambition. First, the book and additional articles for academic journals are published in English. We hope that this will facilitate the interaction between the author and other staff member of the Research Centre on the one hand, and colleagues in other countries on the other hand. Second, the research presented provides a transnational comparison and analysis. Third, the theme of research - environmental studies - is the forefront of tourism research and practice internationally, and publications on these issues usually have many readers. I hope that this will be the case with this book as well.

Svend Lundtorp
Chief of Research
Bornholms Forskningscenter
November 1996

Author's Preface

"Tourism in the Peripheral Areas of Europe" is the title of a research programme financed by the Danish Social Science Research Council. The programme is operated by Bornholms Forskningscenter (Research Centre of Bornholm).

This book is one of the outcomes of the project "Tourism and the Environment - the Innovation Connection", which was initiated by the programme and performed by Anne-Mette Hjalager, Advance/1, the Science Park in Aarhus. As tourism research is a fairly new discipline in Denmark, it has been a matter of great importance to the author to become a member of the group of researchers involved in this field.

The project has been co-financed by the "Football Pool Money", and the author is grateful for the support and enthusiasm expressed by the administrators of the Danish Open Air Council (Friluftsrådet).

A great many people working in the tourism business, in public regulation and planning bodies, and with tourism research on the three case study islands have played major parts in contributing to the outcome of the project. During visits to the islands they have generously spent both time and effort explaining and interpreting, and they have offered valuable assistance by commenting on draft descriptions of the case studies and supplying additional material. The project could never have been performed without their willingness to participate.

The case studies were carried out during 1995 and 1996. Visits to the islands have been crucial for collecting appropriate information, but, particularly in the case of Mallorca and the Isle of Wight, assistance from local universities before, during, and after the visits has been essential.

On Mallorca, it was Marco Antonio Robledo from the Escola de Turisme, Universitat de les Illes Balears, who provided written documentation and offered his assistance interpreting, where necessary. As regards the Isle of Wight, Keith Wilkes (University of Bournemouth) was very helpful in establishing initial contacts on the island.

The interpretation of the project findings (including any shortcomings) is, however, the responsibility of the author.

Ann Hartl-Nielsen of Bornholms Forskningscenter has been of great help to me in practical matters. The manager of the research programme, Professor Stephen Wanhill, has offered moral support at difficult times, when the concept of the project was contested.

Anne-Mette Hjalager
November 1996

CONTENTS

LIST OF FIGURES

LIST OF TABLES

1. Tourism and the environment - an emerging issue

1.1. Introduction

If a frog is thrown into hot water, it will react immediately and make a panic-stricken attempt to leave these hostile surroundings. He will promptly succeed and thereby save his life. The same frog, now thrown into water held at room temperature, feels comfortable and calms down visibly after his initial excitement. If the water temperature is raised degree by degree, the frog will initially feel the beneficial warmth, continue to swim around quite happily, but will steadily become slower and groggier and groggier. As the water temperature is continually rising, the frog's circulation finally breaks down, and it dies in what, in the beginning, had not been such a hostile environment at all[1].

This parable tells us that we are capable of reacting to sudden shock-like changes in the environment. Such things as TV close-ups of dead seals or birds covered in crude oil produce an immediate response. But in daily life many of us seem to suffer from impairment of memory combined with selective repression.

Predominantly, environmental matters have been connected to daily life. Pollution is related to production and transportation rather than leisure activities. This narrow view is, however, being challenged these years, and the impact of tourism and leisure on the environment is increasingly being debated. Simultaneously, the negative effects of constrained environment standards on tourism is an issue which is moving into the awareness of politicians and residents, particularly in locations which are economically dependent on the activities of tourism.

In other words, a sudden response from consumers to degrading environment, will perhaps lead to actions. The research reported in this book is focused on actions, e.g. the regulation which is undertaken by politicians and business associations. A particular emphasis is put on the analysis of the causes and characteristics of regulations, and the impact on the innovative efforts of the tourism industry.

How does this research add to the advances of previous research into tourism and the

---

[1]   Schertler, Walter: Eco-management in tourism in Steinchke, Albert (ed): Umweltorientiertes Management im Tourismus, Europäisches Tourismus Institut an der Universität Trier, 1994, pp 39-55

environment?

Over the past few years, tourism research has to an increasing extent been focusing on environmental studies. Existing and new journals regularly publish articles on sustainable tourism. Numerous conferences and Internet options are being offered to researchers and practitioners, and books are published at great speed. The majority of the work done devotes itself to a better understanding of the nature of the environmental damage caused by the ever increasing inflows of tourists[2].

The analysis of regulatory practice is also becoming more frequent. In particular, such issues as the need to carefully plan development and growth and to manage visitors to nature parks and environmentally sensitive areas have been intensively researched[3]. The effectiveness of managerial instruments has been investigated, so as to provide a good basic understanding of the types of practice needed to achieve environmental objectives. Most often this type of analysis is, however, prescriptive in nature as it highlights good practice and offers operational check lists and suggestions for measures of relevance to

---

2   For instance: Briassoulis, Helen and Jan van der Straaten: Tourism and the environment: An overview in Briassoulis, Helen and Jan van der Straaten: Tourism and the Environment. Regional, Economic and Policy Issues, Kluwer Academic Publishers, Dordrecht, 1992, pp 1-10; Camhis, M. and H. Coccossis: Environment and tourism in island regions in Planning and Administration, Vol 10, No 1 1983, pp 16-23; Farrell, Bryan H. and Dean Runyan: Ecology and Tourism in Annals of Tourism Research, Vol 18, No 1, 1991; Federation of Nature and National Parks in Europe: Loving them to death, Grafeanu, 1993; Mathieson Alister and Geoffrey Wall: Tourism. Economic, Physical and Social Impacts, Longman, Harlow, 1982; Pearce, Douglas: Tourism and environmental research. A review in International Journal of Environmental Studies, Vol 25, 1985, pp 247-255; Pigram, John J.: Environmental Implications of Tourism Development in Annals of Tourism Research, Vol VII, No 4 1980, pp 554-583; and Ravenscroft, Neil: The environmental impact of recreation and tourism development: a review, in European Environment, Vol 2, Part 2, April 1992, pp 8-13.

3   For instance: Dowling, Ross: An environmentally-based planning model for regional tourism development in Journal of Sustainable Tourism, Vol 1, No 1 1993, pp 17-37; Eagles, Paul F.J., Per Nilsen, Manao Kachi and Susan D. Buse: Ecotourism: an annotated bibliography for planners & managers, The Ecotourism Society, North Bennington, Vermont, 1995; Gunn, Clare A.: Environmental Design and Land Use in Ritchie, J.R. Brent and Charles R. Goeldner (eds.): Travel, Tourism and Hospitality Research: A Handbook for Managers and Researchers, New York, 1987, pp 229-252; Inskeep, Edward: Tourism planning. An integrated and sustainable development approach, Van Nostrand Reinhold, NY, 1991 ; Lindberg, Kreg and Hawkins, Donald E. (eds): Ecotourism. A guide for planners and managers, The Ecotourism Society, North Bennington, Vermont, 1993; McIntyre, George: Sustainable tourism development: guide for local planners, WTO, Madrid, 1993; Sidaway, Roger and Han van der Voet: Getting on Speaking terms: resolving conflicts between recreation and nature in coastal zone areas of the Netherlands. A literature study and case study analysis, Landbouwuniversiteit Wageningen, September 1993; and Ziffer, Karen: Ecotourism: An Uneasy Alliance, Conservation International and Ernst & Young, Fall 1989

authorities, managers and visitors.

Another section of studies concentrates on consumer demand. The tourism industry's handling of consumer attitudes and preferences is dealt with in research reports that offer insights into the mechanisms behind the expression of tourists' preferences, and discuss how market demand has a pull-effect on the supply of "green products"[4]. In this way they highlight how regulation takes place by bringing more or less "pure" market forces into play.

The business response to changes in consumer behaviour varies from the "shallow to the deep green", from green labelling to changing agents. Wight raises very crucial questions about the potential of marketing as a moderator[5]. Are tour operators and travel agents serious or are they just faking?

"Self-regulation" is a modern option of importance to a complete understanding of the range of regulatory options. Business self-regulation might be considered essential not only because of its beneficial effect on the environment, but because initiatives of this kind may also be seen as instruments to increase competitiveness and to postpone un-warranted government intervention into business affairs[6].

Accordingly, the bulk of the research that has been performed over the past few years has touched upon many important aspects within the regulation of tourism. Mostly, however, regulation issues are secondary to other research objectives. A more comprehensive interpretation of the composition of regulatory instruments is essential, and this study intends to move in that direction.

---

4   For an overview see for instance: Eadington, William and Valene L. Smith: The emerging of alternative forms of tourism in Smith, Valene L. and William R. Eadington (eds): Tourism alternatives. Potentials and problems in the development of tourism, University of Pen-sylvania Press, Philadelphia, 1992, pp 1-12; Hopfenbeck, Waldemar and Peter Zimmer: Umweltorientiertes Tourismusmanagement. Strategien. Checklisten. Fallstudien, Verlag Moderne Industrie, Landsberg/Lech, 1993; Masterton, Ann M.: Environmental ethics in Harssel, Jan van: Tourism. An exploration. Prentice Hall, Englewood Cliffs, 1994, pp 276-278; and Wight, P: The greening of the hospitality industry: economic and environmental good sense in Seaton, A.V. (ed): Tourism. The state of the art. John Wiley & Sons, Chiche-ster 1994, pp 665-674

5   Wight, P.: Enviromentally responsible marketing of tourism in Cater, Erlet og Gwen Lowman: Ecotourism. A sustainable option? Wiley, Chichester, 1994, pp 39-56

6   WTTERC: Travel and tourism. Environment and development, World Tourism & Travel Review, 1993 outlines these issues, which are given a more general treatment in Elkington, John: The green capitalists, Victor Gollancz, UK, 1989

1.2. Research methodology

Trend-setting organisations are increasingly claiming that the environment will become the key issue in future tourism growth and development[7]. According to these organisations and authorities, a destination that neglects the protection of the environment will loose its visitors to other destinations. Conversely, destinations favoured by a clean environment, or which attempt to obtain and protect high standards, will enjoy continued or increased tourist inflows. Financial issues are often combined with visions of sustainable tourism: tourists with higher incomes, who consequently spend more, tend to choose localities where the environment is well taken care of. Destinations with environmental problems will only be able to appeal to less lucrative markets.

"Smart" stories of this type abound in the travel press. They should therefore be given a closer examination - especially as they represent a popular common-sense view of things. Is it correct that the market reacts immediately to issues such as environmental standards? Do the relevant actors at the destinations seriously consider the challenges? Why? Why not?

To handle what might just be myths and to investigate the processes leading to a more sustainable tourism industry represents an enormous research task. The range of preconditions and consequences is considerable but, fortunately, these days, researchers of many disciplines are willing to allocate resources for further studies. The three case studies reported on here represent only a small corner of the overall issue.

The main priority of this research work is to examine the relation between the environmental imperative on the one hand and business innovations on the other. Innovation studies in tourism are very rare[8], and studies of the effects of environmental regulation on tourism innovations do not exist.

---

7   See, amongst others: Commission of the European Communities: Towards Sustainability. A European Community Programme of Policy and Action in Relation to the Environment and Sustainable Development, March 1992; Eber, Shirley (ed): Beyond the Green Horizon. Principles for Sustainable Tourism, WWF, UK, Godalming, 1992; Hiranyakit, Somchai: Tourism Planning and the Environment in UNEP Industry and Environment, Jan-Mar 1984; and OECD: The Impact of Tourism on the Environment, General Report, Paris, 1980

8   Hjalager, Anne-Mette: Dynamic innovation in the tourism industry in Cooper, C.P and A. Lockwood (eds): Progress in Tourism, Recreation and Hospitality Management, Vol 6, John Wiley & Sons, Chichester, 1994, pp 197-224

In deference to the novelty of the subject, the case studies will serve the following purposes:

- *Exploration.* The issue of sustainable tourism has become a popular one, and in recent years much has been written. However, the major part of the material supplied by researchers and organisations tends to be normative and prescriptive, rather than analytical. Besides, many aspects have not been studied, e.g the link with innovations. Accordingly, the research work performed has had to identify, describe and classify typical cases of environment-innovation links in an explorative way.

- *Explanation.* As far at possible, this type of research will attempt to answer the questions of "why" and "how". In particular, the role played by the public regulations governing the innovative activities is crucial to this project, but other mechanisms such as demand changes, variations in regional conditions, and the diffusion of trade behavioral "best practice" models will also be included in the explanatory discussion.

- *Theory.* The conclusions of this study will need to be discussed in relation to an innovation theory framework previously provided[9]. Necessary modifications or expansions of the framework will be undertaken. In addition, other theoretical traditions will have to be included in order to fulfil the explanatory purpose, e.g. regulation theories.

The hypotheses that will be challenged during the research process thus read as follows:

- The tourism industry is changing its products, processes, organisational set-up, and marketing approach *in response* to an observed and anticipated environmental disequilibrium, threat, or change in consumer demands.

- The intensity and direction which innovations take vary according to the activities of the enterprises, their ownership, size, inclusion in regional business milieux, and the degree and mode of public intervention.

- How, when and why authorities choose to intervene in the operations of tourist enterprises has a decisive influence on the scope and scale of the innovations. Public regulations are thus important mechanisms that not only

---

9   Ibid; Hjalager, Anne-Mette: Tourism and the environment - the innovation connection in Journal of Sustainable Tourism, forthcoming; and Hjalager, Anne-Mette: Innovation patterns in sustainable tourism - an analytical typology in Tourism Management, Vol 18, No 1, 1997

ensure certain environmental standards, but (more importantly for this project) also influence the occurrence and diffusion of innovations.

The objective is to deepen - by means of case studies - the understanding of innovative mechanisms, and - if needed - to modify the hypotheses.

Case studies represent only one of many ways of acquiring information in social science. Other methods which might be mentioned include surveys, documentation based on literature, and investigations of data sets held by authorities or organisations. As noted by Yin[10]:

"A case study is an empirical inquiry that:

- investigates a contemporary phenomenon within its real-life context; when

- the boundaries between the phenomenon and context are not clearly evident; and

- multiple sources of evidence are used". (p 23)

As there are major explanatory and exploratory tasks to be solved, the subject of this research project fits in well with the basic conditions inherent in the case study method. At this stage surveys would not be appropriate, as precise questions cannot yet be formulated.

The advantages of the case study method that can be identified for this particular type of research are:

Firstly, the contextual framework of the phenomenon being studied is crucial to the understanding not only of what type of activity is taking place, but also of "how" and "why" environmental stresses and opportunities affect the innovativeness of the tourism industry. The research undertaken here will have to explain and make plausible the causal links (or the lack of causal links) between industrial behaviour and the surrounding push factors, in particular the regulatory forces.

Secondly, it is evident that, in the case of tourism, the environment may be said to be an issue with non-distinctive boundaries. Tourism and tourists are not the only ones to cause pollution, and both the tourists and the local population are affected by it.

---

10   Yin, Robert K.: Case study research. Design and methods, Applied Social Research Methods
        Series, Vol. 5, Sage Publications, Newbury Park, 1989

Accordingly, environmental policies rarely aim to change the behaviour of tourists or tourist enterprises exclusively. The contextual framework is therefore of particular importance, and the case study method represents the natural choice.

Thirdly, the nature of the sources relevant in this type of study also points towards the case study method rather than other methods. Interviews with several different groups of people are essential, but the interviews have to be supplemented with observations and an analysis of documents.

In addition, the following advantages of the case study method, adapted from Merriam, are relevant in relation to this type of research:

- The inductive research strategy makes it possible to collect and operate variables which were not obvious during the planning phase of the study. This does not, however, render careful planning any less necessary.

- It is possible to show the complexity of a phenomenon, and so indicate that not just one factor is influencing certain change processes and situations.

- The focus is on the important role played by human behaviour and personal action during change processes.

- It may illustrate the time dimension involved in change processes; the occurrence and effects of development over time.

- It will help explain why a particular problem appeared in the first place.

- It is the only mode capable of comprehensively explaining the reasons for certain actions and the reasons for the success or failure of these actions[11].

As pointed out by Yin, there are many objections to the case study methodology. The most extensively used argument is that the results reached by means of such a study are not representative. Yin counters this argument by stating that "..case studies - like experiments - are generalizable to theoretical propositions and not to populations or universes. In this sense, the case study, like the experiment, does not represent a "sample", and the investigator's goal is to expand and generalize theories (analytic generalization) and not to enumerate frequencies (statistical generalization)" (p 21).

In this study, the exploratory and explanatory elements are in focus as are modifications

---

11   Merriam, Sharan: Fallstudien som forskningsmetod, Studentlitteratur, Lund, 1994

and expansions of theories and models. There are therefore no extensive requirements as to the provision of a distinct representative quality. In future research work, the categories devised for this study will perhaps be useful in connection with surveys and other types of quantitative research methods.

1.3. Purpose of the case studies

As pointed out earlier, innovation in tourism has only been scantily investigated. Case studies will thus be of great importance for establishing research into innovation in this particular sector more firmly, e.g. by applying it to a specific theme - the environment.

The emphasis will be placed on the following targets:

- To identify examples of innovative activities of public, semi-public and private institutions or the networks formed by these partners within such categories of innovation as process, product, managerial/organisational and distributional innovations. The radicalness of the innovations will be analysed against the nature of environmental problems, political inclinations and external change catalysts.

- To classify the regulatory systems adopted by the authorities in charge of tourism and the environment. The theoretical framework established by Ouchi will form the terms of reference for this analysis, e.g. A: The market as regulator through price mechanisms, B: Bureaucracies regulating by legal and planning measures, C: Clan - regulation by business organisations and voluntary networks[12].

A brief outline of the types and intensity of the environmental stresses existing in three different regions serves as the necessary background information for the analysis. This will assist the interpretation and discussion of the differences observed in the scale and scope of the innovations and in the regulatory systems chosen for this study.

Even more important in relation to this study, however, is the identification of the next link in the chain:

---

12   Ouchi, William G.: Markets, bureaucracies and clans in Administrative Science Quarterly, Vol 25, March 1980, pp 129-141

- How do individual tourist enterprises or groups of tourist enterprises react (if they do) to regulations and to initiatives launched by the "extra-parliamentary policy initiator", e.g. the transformation of an external stress or demand situation into a competitive advantage by way of innovative efforts.

The explanatory parts of this case study also draw on a comparison of three regions as a particularly crucial element.

1.4. Regulation and innovation - a model

A schematic outline of the case studies is provided below.

As shown in the model, the causal relations are of particular importance to the study. But they will not make any sense unless coupled with the fact-finding questions included in the boxes.

Figure 1.1: Model of analysis

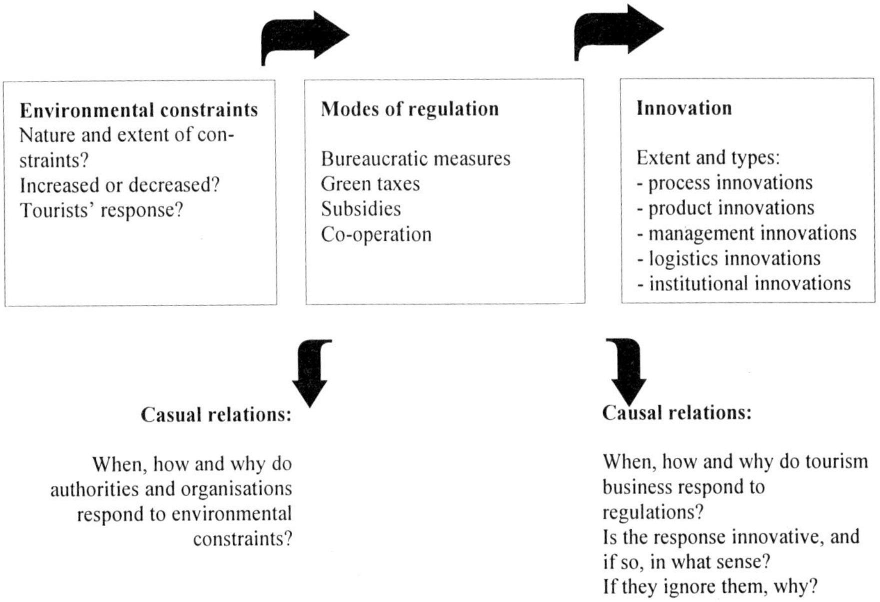

| **Environmental constraints** Nature and extent of constraints? Increased or decreased? Tourists' response? | **Modes of regulation** Bureaucratic measures Green taxes Subsidies Co-operation | **Innovation** Extent and types: - process innovations - product innovations - management innovations - logistics innovations - institutional innovations |

Casual relations:

When, how and why do authorities and organisations respond to environmental constraints?

Causal relations:

When, how and why do tourism business respond to regulations? Is the response innovative, and if so, in what sense? If they ignore them, why?

1.5. Choice of case study regions

This research project forms part of a major research programme entitled "Tourism in peripheral areas of Europe". The Danish core region included in the research programme is the island of Bornholm in the Baltic Sea. This island has a population of about 45,000 and a long tradition of tourism. Parts of the research undertaken under this programme will use Bornholm as a study region, thus taking advantage of the co-operative networks of researchers investigating different aspects.

Bornholm was thus chosen a priori as a case study region.

Two comparable regions in Europe had to be found for similar case studies. The following preliminary selection criteria were set up:

- Regions should be comparable in size and population to Bornholm (a fairly wide margin allowed).

- The existence of regional policy-making units was of crucial importance. The islands should not be (entirely) governed from the mainland or larger regions.

- One island to be located preferably in the UK/Ireland, another in southern Europe.

- The islands should preferably be places where other researchers are or were involved in sustainable tourism issues, so as to enable an exchange of information, data and opinions.

It has been difficult to find islands fulfilling all these criteria. As a compromise the Isle of Wight in the UK and Mallorca in Spain were thus chosen for case studies.

1.6. Planning of the case studies

The following process has been applied in each of the case studies:

- Collection of data and material from secondary sources.

- Preparation of interview guides aimed at public authorities, NGOs and private tourism enterprises.

- Appointments with key persons in the public authorities responsible for the promotion of tourism and those responsible for planning and environmental protection. Predominantly civil servants were selected for these interviews.

- Appointments with key persons from selected NGOs and trade organisations and from important or particularly environmentally aware tourist enterprises.

- Viewing of sites at critical places pointed out by the interviewees.

- Collection of supplementary secondary material, additional telephone calls with other informants.

- Drafting of first version of case study report.

- Comments on the draft from interviewees and other key persons.

- Inclusion of the revised versions of the case study reports in sections 2-4 of this book.

For this book, it was considered important to integrate the case studies into the theoretical framework, particularly theory on innovation and on the types and impacts of public regulation on the sustainability of tourism. Chapter five is dedicated to testing the theoretical concepts and terms, and a discussion of the validity of the theories.

2. Bornholm

2.1. Introduction

This case study is concerned with tourism and the environment on Bornholm as well as with its impact on innovation in the tourism business sector of the island.

Firstly, a brief description outlining how important tourism is to the island will be provided, including comparisons with other economic sectors and activities. The following section will describe the extent and nature of the environmental constraints existing on the island, in particular constraints relating to tourism. Tourism is, however, not the only sector to affect the environment, and it is not possible to allot it any clear responsibility. This issue will be a matter for discussion.

In section 2.4. the environmental regulation system on Bornholm will be outlined. The concept of environmental regulation used covers a broad range, so as to be able to include public planning and legal regulation as well as business "self-regulation", codexes and other more voluntary actions aimed at the alleviation of environmental problems.

Innovations devised in answer to environmental problems and regulations will be analysed in section 2.5., which also includes a conclusion summing up the specific issues affecting the sustainability of tourism on Bornholm.

2.2. The importance of tourism to the island

Bornholm is located in the Baltic Sea. As the crow flies the distance to Copenhagen measures 160 kilometres, while the distance to the southern coast of Sweden is 40 kilometres. A distance of nearly 100 kilometres separates Bornholm from Poland, and the same distance has to be travelled to reach Rügen in Germany.

Bornholm covers an area of 590 square kilometres and has a population of 45,000. Since 1980 the population has dropped by 6.5 per cent, predominantly because young people want to go to the mainland for further education. The population did, however, stop declining in 1994-1995.

The development of tourism on Bornholm is illustrated in Figure 2.1.

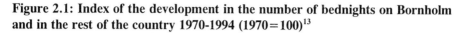

Figure 2.1: Index of the development in the number of bednights on Bornholm and in the rest of the country 1970-1994 (1970=100)[13]

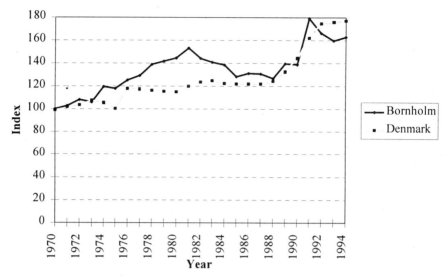

It can be observed that the number of tourist bednights has risen over the period from 1970 to 1994. There is no doubt that in a Danish context Bornholm is a significant tourist destination with the number of bednights per year totalling 2.36 million (1994). The development that has taken place over the years is comparable to that which has taken place in Denmark as a whole, particularly in the 1980s.

When it comes to development by accommodation types, distinctive variations can be found, as illustrated in Figure 2.2.

13   Sources: Rafn, Thomas: Turismens økonomiske betydning for Bornholm, Bornholms
        Forskningscenter, 1995; and Jensen, Susanne: Turismens økonomiske betydning i Danmark i
        1991, Institut for grænseregionsforskning, Åbenrå, 1993

Figure 2.2.: Index of the development in tourism bednights by types of accommodation, 1987-1994

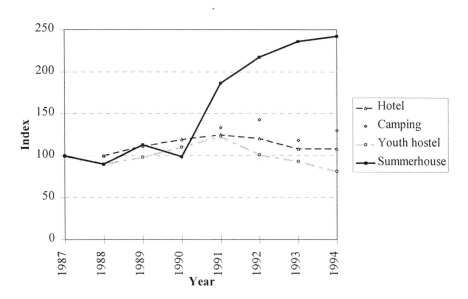

A boom has taken place in the nights spent in summer houses (holiday homes). This trend is identical to the situation in the rest of Denmark. Over the last decade, more and more privately owned summer houses have been put up for rent. In addition, the tax authorities have been very keen to record the degree to which these houses were rented out, thus perhaps leading to their inclusion as bednights in the tourist statistics which were compiled earlier. It is, however, a matter of fact that Danish tourism has moved towards higher volumes of self-catering accommodation, which to an increasing extent is considered "value for money" by tourists visiting Denmark.

Many hotels reacted to this trend by converting traditional rooms into apartments. Accordingly, hotel statistics also include some self-catering accommodation.

The bednights spent in summer houses account for half of the total number of bednights on Bornholm. Hotels follow right behind, while camping and youth hostels are of more marginal importance. Visits to friends and relatives are not included in the figures, but Rafn estimates them at around 400,000 bednights per year[14].

---

14   Rafn, Thomas: Turismens økonomiske betydning for Bornholm, Bornholms Forsknings-
        center, 1995

The most significant markets for Bornholm are Germany, the rest of Denmark, and Sweden. As shown in Figure 2.3, the inflow from other countries is very low.

Figure 2.3.: Number of bednights by nationality, 1992-1994[15]

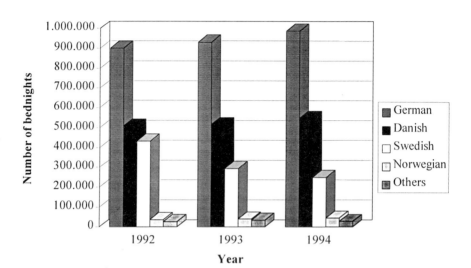

The long and expensive ferry (or flight) trip to Bornholm renders the island very vulnerable to changes in the economic conditions on these markets. This was rather dramatically the case in 1993, which was the season following the devaluation of the Swedish currency.

Bornholm is a "cold water" destination, and therefore seasonal fluctuations are pronounced, as illustrated in Figure 2.4.

---

15   Source: Dandata. Visits to friends and relatives are not included

Figure 2.4. Bednights on Bornholm, by month, 1994[16]

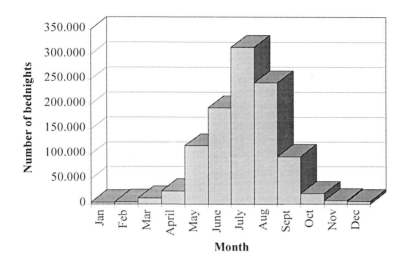

During the three summer months Bornholm accommodates 55 times as many tourists as during the three winter months and three times as many as during the shoulder seasons in the spring and autumn.

How dependent is Bornholm's population on tourism activities? It is difficult to make any precise distinctions between the tourism industry and other economic sectors. An analysis based on labour market statistics[17] confirmed that around 2,000 out of 22,000 jobs (full-time or part-time jobs) were to be found in the tourism and leisure sectors (1990). Another result of the same analysis was that over a period of ten years, a 60% increase in the number of jobs in tourism and leisure could be demonstrated. This is a very considerable increase compared to other tourist destinations in Denmark.

16   Source: Dandata. The figure includes hotels, camping and youth hostels

17   Holm-Petersen, Erik, Anne-Mette Hjalager, Wolfgang Framke and Peter Plougmann: Turisme/fritid - en erhvervsøkonomisk analyse, Erhvervsfremme Styrelsen, København, 1993

Rafn employs another method of estimating the number of jobs in tourism[18]. His method results in a lower number: 1,114. Rafn's calculations only include full-time jobs, which will account for some of the difference. The job impact of the purchases made by the local population in restaurants, etc. has not been included in Rafn's totals, either.

Rafn also calculated the local economy's income from tourism. This accounts for DKK 1.23 million, or 5.3 per cent of the island's Gross Factor Income. The income from tourism earned by the Danish economy as a whole, amounts to only 1.5 per cent of GFI, which illustrates Bornholm's higher dependency on tourism in comparison with the rest of the country.

It may be concluded that tourism accounts for only a relatively small proportion of direct and indirect employment and income on Bornholm, but the dependency on this sector is slightly more pronounced than in other parts of Denmark. Tourism must, however, not be regarded as an isolated matter. Other job and income opportunities, particularly in the fishing and fish processing industry, have been reduced over a period of time. Between 1987 and 1992, 27 per cent of the jobs in the fish processing industry disappeared[19], and tourism cannot be expected to replace them all. Also within the agricultural sector manpower requirements continue to decline. Unemployment rates are around 12 per cent. Emigration and a growth in the public sector has helped to keep unemployment at a level comparable to the Danish average.

Over the last decade, tourism has created jobs for people on Bornholm. The population and the politicians still have confidence in the future opportunities of tourism. Policy programmes include measures to increase earnings and job creation based on tourism. To this end instruments have been introduced[20] which aim at higher quality products and longer seasons.

To conclude - Bornholm is a significant tourist destination in Denmark, and as such it appeals predominantly to tourists from the neighbouring markets. Tourism's impact on incomes and employment does not justify the claim that Bornholm is to a very large extent dependent on tourism. Heavy seasonal fluctuations require the population to be alert in relation to other opportunities. Its importance has, however, increased as jobs in others sector have disappeared, and in the future more emphasis is likely to be put on

---

18   Rafn, Thomas: Turismens økonomiske betydning for Bornholm, Bornholms Forsknings-
        center, 1995 and Rafn, Thomas: Turismens betydning for de danske amter, Bornholms
        Forskningscenter, Nexø, 1996

19   Bornholms Amt: Regionplan, 1993, Rønne, 1994

20   Bornholms Amt: Regionplan, 1993, Rønne, 1994

the promotion of tourism.

When the particular characteristics of tourism on Bornholm are linked to environmental issues, the following points should be emphasized:

- The mere fact of the high numbers of tourists is often underlined as a very important environmental factor. Bornholm has a higher "tourist density" than most other areas in Denmark[21]. Whether the high number of tourists constitutes a genuine environmental constraint should, however, only be evaluated in relation to the carrying capacity of the island. Section 2.3. will discuss these proportions in greater detail.

- At the height of the season there are nearly as many tourists as residents. Among other things this means that the capacity of the waste water and solid waste handling services and of the drinking water supply system must be adapted to higher numbers of users. In addition, the wear and tear on flora, fauna and infrastructure is very unevenly distributed over the year.

- A large proportion of tourists are Germans. In relation to environmental matters this should be considered an advantage, as public opinion in Germany is moving fast towards higher environmental awareness and more considerate behaviour[22].

- Increasingly, tourists want to experience comfort. In general, this leads to a higher consumption of energy, water and other resources. Bornholm is no exception, although primitive camping and accommodation in youth hostels still enjoy some popularity. The fact that tourism is concentrated in the summer season does, however, limit the demand for heating energy.

Taking these statistically based characteristics into consideration, tourism on Bornholm cannot be claimed to result in any particular environmental constraints. In order to widen the perspective, one must, however, analyze other elements as well.

---

21   Framke, Wolfgang: Turismens belastning af miljøet in Turisme nr 8, 1993

22   Hopfenbeck, Waldemar and Peter Zimmer: Umweltorientiertes Tourismusmanagement. Strategien. Checklisten. Fallstudien. Verlag Moderne Industri, 1993

2.3. The nature and extent of environmental constraints

The presence of tourists has an effect on the environment that is mostly but not entirely negative. On the other hand, the non-existence of environmental protection measures may affect tourism, no matter whether the constraints are a result of tourism or of other activities. This analysis of the scope and scale of environmental constraints looks into the following subjects:

- Changes in landscapes and towns
- Consumption of drinking water
- Waste water
- Noise
- Solid waste
- Energy consumption.

2.3.1. Changes in landscapes and towns

Tourists to Bornholm are active people. The landscapes and natural resources are very important attractions. Based on a survey among tourists in summer houses Bornholm's Welcome Centre concludes that 62% of the tourists come because of the natural resources[23]. Munch-Petersen[24] emphasizes this aspect in a more recent survey including all groups of tourists to Bornholm.

Larger numbers of tourists are bound to influence nature and landscapes, but on Bornholm planning measures have been adopted in an attempt to keep the built-up environment within existing boundaries. Uncontrolled sprawl has not taken place. The growth in tourism is the result of the increased number of summer houses being rented out, thus making it possible to accommodate the major part of the additional tourist inflow in already existing capacity - with the exception of minor expansions of the summer house districts.

Some hotels and camp sites have extended their facilities, but lack of market demand has limited this activity. Sites set aside for new hotels and camping establishments have not, in fact been built on.

The overall effect of tourism expansion on landscape resources is limited; changes in

---

23   Hasløv og Kjærsgaard: Notat vedr. spørgeskemaundersøgelsen 1994, February 1995

24   Munch-Petersen, Nils Finn: The Bornholm vacation product, research paper, Bornholms Forskningscenter, March 1996

landscapes and towns are not connected to the erection of new accommodation facilities. The activities of tourists visiting the area will, however, have environmental consequences and the environment will also be affected by the activities of others. The debate on the island concentrates on the following:

The beaches. There are several sources for the pollution of the beaches. In certain areas - particularly along the south coast with high tourism densities - there have been many problems with seaweed. When seaweed is washed ashore it goes into decay and thus causes obnoxious smells and aesthetic disturbances. The natural types of seaweed have been displaced by algae which are better able to exploit high contents of nutrients in the sea[25]. The occurrence of these algae is not solely due to the tourists. They are the combined result of the tourists', the residents' and agriculture's discharges of nutrients. The County Council states that while problems with agricultural discharges are still grave, problems with waste water from towns and settlements are now being solved[26].

Another very visible problem encountered on the beaches is the solid waste and waste oil discharged from ships in the Baltic Sea. Waste paper, etc. on the beaches constitutes a minor problem, which is solely the responsibility of the tourists and residents.

The towns. Towns such as Rønne, Svaneke, Gudhjem and Allinge are popular places for excursions because they are picturesque and beautifully situated in the landscape. In the high season, the pressure on these towns is very great, but there are no indications that the tourists find them too crowded. The permanent residents tend to think that the pressure in the season is uncomfortably high. In most towns and villages traffic and parking problems are severe during July and August.

A number of shops and restaurants are only open during the high season. Often their visual appearance has not been very well adapted to the style of the town, and closed facades during the off-season are not very appealing. A fast turnover in the ownership of these types of businesses tends to aggravate the problem.

Nature and landscapes. Bornholm is well supplied with natural resources. The largest part of the island is utilized for agricultural purposes; agricultural areas amounting to 69 per cent of the total. Twenty-one per cent of the island is covered with forests, and 3 per cent remains uncultivated[27].

---

25   Bornholms Amt: Vandmiljøet på Bornholm, Resultater af 5 års overvågning, n.d.

26   Bornholms Amt: Energy and Environment, 1992

27   Bornholms Amt: Regionplan 1993, Rønne, February 1994

Compared with the rest of Denmark, the forested areas occupy twice as much space as anywhere else. The largest forests, located in the centre of the island, are characterized by very varied scenery with lakes, marshes, rift valleys, and enclaves with deciduous forest, heather and scrub. Remains of original hornbeam woods can be found. Usually each farm has its own small plantation which adds a specific feature to the landscape. Forested areas can also be found along the coast. They consist mainly of Scots pine and birch[28]. As these woodland areas are usually fully accessible to tourists, who can use them for walking, cycling and riding, the recreational resources of the island must be regarded as considerable. But in fact, the tourists tend to concentrate their activities on selected roads and trails and on smaller areas of the island. Accordingly, erosion and other types of disturbances are very rarely observed, except in the key attraction areas such as Hammershus and Paradisbakkerne.

Some areas contain particularly vulnerable flora and fauna, which could not possibly survive a massive invasion. There are no access regulations, but the authorities do not inform the public of the location of these areas. So far this lack of information has turned out to be sufficient when it comes to protection.

Bornholm is the only area in Denmark with a rock subsurface. In the past, the extraction industry was very important, and extraction still takes place. Over the next few decades, a number of quarries will be closed down and transferred to recreational purposes, thus expanding the resources and the variety of landscapes available to tourism and leisure.

Some of the rocky coastal areas and overhangs are popular for climbing and hang-gliding. The protection lobby on the island is anxious that these activities may disturb the wildlife and destroy the vulnerable and sparse vegetation.

Angling is dependent on the existence of a population of fish, especially a significant species such as the sea trout. To some extent anglers compete for the fish population with the artisanal fishing sector. The need for regulation has become evident on Bornholm, and in addition the authorities are now launching projects which will increase the fish population - a fact which is to the advantage of both groups.

Rock climbing and angling are the only leisure activities that have caused manifest conflicts over the last decade. The County Council has investigated all leisure activities (cycling, riding, windsurfing, rowing/canoeing, sailing, hunting and angling) and it was found that intensified activities will increase the need for planning, so that conflicts and

---

28   Bornholms Amt: Tillæg til regionplan 1985 om skovrejsning, December 1991

environmental damage may be avoided[29].

2.3.2. Fresh water supply

Until 1989 the consumption of ground water was rising on Bornholm. After that time it has been possible to reduce consumption to the level of the mid-1970s. Closures and changed processes in the fish processing industries are two reasons for this. In addition, the suppliers (predominantly the municipalities) have actively renovated the distribution network, and introduced water-saving measures such as water meters. The water consumed by tourism has not been estimated, and the willingness of tourists to save water is not documented. Higher accommodation standards are likely to increase the consumption of water. Nevertheless, the County Council expects a further decline in the consumption of water on the island.

Ground water is a scarce resource which is difficult to obtain on Bornholm. On top of this, ground water resources are threatened by harmful substances escaping from land fills and industrial sites, and a surplus of pesticides and nutrients from agriculture is bound also to compromise the quality of drinking water. The leaching of nitrates and nitrogens from fertilizers represents an increasing problem, and might, in the long run, affect the possibilities of obtaining drinking water. Measures have been taken to protect certain drinking water supply zones.

Tourism does not directly cause any pollution of drinking water. But an enlarged summer population increases the amount of water that has to be pumped to the surface. Although only marginally so, this might add to the lowering of the water table and to any risks of penetration of unwanted substances, for instance salt.

The fresh water supply is recognized as a critical factor on Bornholm, and the water management plan[30] represents a proactive attempt at avoiding emergencies. However, agricultural policies are not a matter for the regional authorities.

2.3.3. Waste water treatment

Previously, waste water was discharged directly into the sea. As the currents around the island bring about rapid dispersal of the waste, this was found to be an acceptable solution. However, the national water quality plan of 1987 changed the concept of waste

---

29   Bornholms Amt: Friluftslivets interesseområder, Rønne, 1984

30   Bornholms Amt: Vandplan Bornholm

water management. A very ambitious investment programme was launched on Bornholm in order to ensure the treatment of all waste water from towns and industries.

In 1994 and 1995 the discharge of untreated waste water has been dramatically reduced. The investment programme will be completed in 1998, and by then practically no waste water will be allowed to flow into the Baltic Sea untreated. The treatment will then be of secondary level and beyond[31].

Areas with a concentration of tourists are to be included in the water treatment program-mes. Exceptions are some of the summer house areas which are not connected to sewer systems. The authorities do not regard this as a problem because of the short season and the particular location of the areas.

Tourists do contribute to the generation of waste water, but the development of the treatment systems will result in a situation where this will no longer have to be considered a critical matter.

In spite of generally good levels of bathing water quality and higher levels of waste water treatment, a few places did not meet the standards as recently as in 1995. In general, the municipalities do not want to adopt the Blue Flag concept, predominantly because the requirements that have to be met in regard to beach facilities are considered excessive.

2.3.4. Noise

Noise has to be considered a very small problem only marginally affecting tourism on Bornholm. A survey shows, however, that summer houses located in the neighbourhood of the airport are considered less attractive[32]. In a few locations, conflicts caused by noise from restaurants and discotheques have been discussed in the press.

Noisy leisure activities, such as riding water scooters, are not allowed near the coast. Shooting takes place in areas dedicated to the purpose, and tourists do not often participate in this type of leisure activity.

Tourists on Bornholm only contribute marginally to the creation of offensive noises - and they are fairly undisturbed by noise created by others.

---

31   Bornholms Amt: Spildevand 1994, 1995

32   Hasløv and Kjærsgaard: Notat vedr. spørgeskemaundersøgelsen 1994, February 1995

34

2.3.5. Solid waste treatment

Solid waste is generated at a number of stages and places:

- In summer houses, where the waste is comparable to ordinary household waste. However, purchasing such articles as fast food, beach toys, etc. often leads to higher amounts of discarded packaging than is the case in ordinary households. Tourists are in no position to ensure that their organic waste is composted, and the burning of solid waste is not permitted. BOFA (the waste treatment company) has calculated that the solid waste generated amounts to 575 grammes per day per inhabitant. Another investigation shows that the amounts of solid waste generated in tourist areas are somewhat higher, and that this amount rose by 130 per cent over a period of eight years[33].

- Normally hotels, resorts, restaurants and camp sites are large enterprises with a centralised treatment and separation of solid waste. There is no information about the total amount of waste from these types of establishments[34]. An estimate from Hotel Balka Strand shows that one guest will produce up to 1.3 kilos of waste per day[35].

- Waste is generated in connection with ferry and air transportion, in particular the packaging for tax free products and catering. The ferry companies deliver this waste to be processed by the waste treatment plant on the island. Because of the Danish recycled bottle system, there are no treatment facilities for aluminium drink containers, which often form part of the tax free assortment.

- On the transit routes from the ferries to the place of accommodation, tourists often attempt to get rid of solid waste. Lay-bys do not always have the necessary facilities to be able to cope with the large number of cars leaving the ferries.

---

33   Rambøll, Hannemann and Højlund: Tourist project no 9. Environmental analysis of summer houses/holiday houses, Esbjerg, July 1994

34   For instance in HORECON: Afrapportering af forprojekt: "Bornholm - en ø med miljøbevidst turisme", 1995. However, Hopfenbeck and Zimmer (1993) note that a hotel guest generates 2.8 litres of solid waste per day, and a restaurant guest generates 1.6 litres per meal. The authors claim that these amounts could be reduced to 1.6 and 1.0 litres, respectively. (Hopfenbeck, Waldemar and Peter Zimmer: Umweltorientiertes Tourismusmanagement. Strategien, Checklisten, Fallstudien, Verlag Moderne Industrie, Landsberg/Lech, 1993)

35   Nexø kommune: Delrapport om projekt KURS, 21 July 1994

Many tourists and representatives from the local tourist associations see the solid waste treatment system as a problem, in spite of the fact that treatment and recycling is very well developed on the island. These problems are of a practical nature, and all have their origin in the (non-)availability of information. Waste is not collected on Saturdays, the usual day for the arrival of new guests at the summer houses. New guests may thus be greeted by un-emptied dustbins. This is considered a symptom indicating that the environment is not being properly taken care of. The treatment plant claims that the summer house owners are disinclined to pay for extra collections of waste.

Recycling only includes certain items, for instance bottles, paper and batteries. The solid waste treatment plant cannot handle any more fragments and does not want to ask for further separation of the waste than necessary. At home, German tourists are used to separation into more fragments, and they find the Danish systems insufficient.

BOFA - the treatment plant - undertakes the incineration and recycling of the bulk of the household waste. Land fills are used for a very small amount of waste which cannot be recycled elsewhere. The incineration process generates heat for the district heating system of the town of Rønne. As the tourist season is also the season with lowest demands on the district heating system, the treatment plant has to keep waste in stock during the summer for later use.

The non-handling of this waste is very easily turned into a visible problem, causing residents and tourists to think that the systems in place on Bornholm are insufficient. Paradoxically therefore the handling of waste is a major issue in the environmental debate, because information and logistics seem to fail. This happens in spite of the fact that the island has a very advanced treatment system which serves as a demonstration system throughout Europe.

2.3.6. Energy comsumption

In 1984 Jørgensen et al estimated that tourism on Bornholm accounted for an energy consumption of 46 GWh per year, which is the equivalent of 3.5 per cent of the total energy consumption on the island[36]. This estimate did not include retail services, which are also at the disposal of the residents. Since 1984 tourism has increased by 18%, and in the same period some energy consuming industries have reduced their activities or introduced saving measures. Thus, today tourism's share of the energy consumption is

---

36   Jørgensen, Kaj, Nielsen I. Meyer and Henning Pilegaard: Energiplan for en grøn ø, Borgen, 1986.

probably higher than 3.5 per cent.

Tourists consume energy for heating, hot water, electricity and transportation. The emissions arising out of this consumption of energy are of environmental concern. In this respect the seasonality of tourism must be regarded as a positive factor, as the use of heating and electric light is at a minimum.

However, other aspects contribute negatively to the environmental balance:

- Many summer houses are old and insufficiently insulated. This will, however, not have any important consequences unless the houses are inhabited/rented out during the winter period.

- Summer houses come with a range of modern household equipment. In addition, the average size is increasing, which might lead to higher consumption levels.

- Most tourist accommodation (hotels, summer houses) is located outside the district heating areas. From an environmental point of view district heating (particularly when based on incineration or biogas) is better than electric heaters or central heating.

Bornholms Forskningscenter conducts a passenger survey which also includes questions about the main methods used when travelling around on the island[37]. The general impression is that the majority of tourists arrive by ferry, bringing their own car. The ferry companies do not distinguish between tourists and other categories of travellers; neither do the airlines, with the exception of (the very few) charter trips.

The ferry companies operate conventional ferries of a fairly high average age. Only one jetfoil route has been established, but the "Bornholmstrafikken" company considers switching to the faster types of ferries. This will increase energy comsumption per passenger/kilometre by several hundred per cent.

BAT (the regional public transport company) offers tickets which are valid for one week or one day and quantity discount tickets valid for five single days. These types of tickets are often used by tourists, but also by residents. In 1994, BAT sold tickets equivalent to 23,000 days. This should be compared to the total number of tourist days which has been calculated at 2.3 million, a figure which may serve to illustrate the fact that public transport plays a minor role in tourist transportation.

---

37   Unpublished data from the tourist survey 3rd quarter 1995, Bornholms Forskningscenter

It should be observed that Bornholm is an important bicycle tourism destination. Thirty per cent of tourists use their own or a rented bicycle while they are visiting the island[38]. It is estimated that around 177,000 bednights per year can be attributed to tourists who use the bicycle as their only means of transport. A large number of tourists make occasional use of a bicycle, but the bicycle is not the only means of transport [39]. Cycling contributes to a higher degree of sustainability, but its total contribution to transportation is still rather limited.

2.3.7. Conclusions

The environmental constraints and potential constraints of importance to tourism on Bornholm are concentrated on the following issues:

- Water consumption. Tourism is, however, not the only, nor even the most important activity influencing the future prospects of this resource. If managed according to the water supply plans, this resource will be sufficiently available even if a growth in tourism should occur.

- Solid waste treatment. This is considered critical because of the lack of infor- mation and the failing logistics of collection. From a technical point of view the island is running one of the most advanced types of waste treatment plant in Europe.

- Transport. Energy consuming transportation is necessary, because of the remote location of the island, and because private cars are a dominant mode of transport on the island.

- Energy consumption in hotels and summer houses is not at an optimum level.

- The natural resources and landscapes in a few locations on the island are suffering from over heavy inflows. Leisure activities such as angling and rock climbing cause some, but no excessive regulation problems.

These environmental constraints must not be considered too serious. Larger tourism inflows or a heavier concentration in the season may, however, increase the need to

---

38   Unpublished data from the tourist survey 3rd quarter 1995, Bornholms Forskningscenter

39   Simonsen, Peter Saabye and Birgitte Jørgensen: Cykelturisme. Økonomisk og miljømæssig bæredygtighed?, Bornholms Forskningscenter, 1996

regulate in the areas mentioned above.

In two respects tourism on Bornholm is negatively affected by environmental constraints caused by the activities of other economic sectors:

- Agriculture contributes to a declining marine environment, causing growth of algae near the beaches. In addition, agriculture is responsible for some obnoxious smells during the season.

- Oil and solid waste from ships in the Baltic Sea occasionally influence the quality of the beaches and the bathing water.

2.4. The environmental regulation system

2.4.1. Authorities

The Danish system governing the administration of the environment is based on the philosophy of subsidiarity and decentralisation. The decision-making process and the actual physical operation of the system is left to the regional and local authorities as far as this it at all possible. And what is more - the environment is a matter of political commitment, rather than a matter of pure administrative procedure.

This philosophy will explain the division of labour among the three levels: government, county councils and municipalities. This division of labour has not been fundamentally revised since the early 1970s, when environmental legislation was first adopted.

The superior authority is the Parliament. Preparations for political decisions are made in the Committee for the Environment and Planning. The Government, the Parliament and the Committee is assisted by the Ministry for the Environment and Energy. The ministry will draft bills and regulations, will research and evaluate, work out guidelines for the counties and municipalities, and, in some cases, control the activities of the regional and local governments. Two impartial bodies solve disputes arising out of the administration of acts and regulations. Some other ministries are in charge of affairs which are closely connected to the environment, that is the Ministries of Agriculture, Transportation and Trade and Industry.

The counties have a considerable responsibility in regard to the environment. Planning and regulation of the open land and the water resources are issues which are in the hands of the county councils. The county will also co-ordinate the planning and regulation activities undertaken by the municipalities, and provide comprehensive planning documents, a framework within which the municipalities are obliged to operate. The county council controls and issues approvals to the most polluting activities and industries, and sees to the solution of environmental tasks which go beyond municipal boundaries. Over the past decade this state of affairs has resulted in the concentration of a large number of environmental obligations at county level, whereas relatively few obligations have to be fulfilled at the national and municipal levels.

The municipalities (of which there are five on Bornholm) are in charge of local planning. The control and approval of discharges, for instance those caused by agricultural holdings and manufacturing industries, are also a local task. As in regional planning, the municipalities must prepare comprehensive and co-ordinated plans, where the inclusion of environmental considerations has become increasingly important. Usually, the municipalities will operate the water and energy supply systems and the waste and waste water handlings systems. In many cases the municipalities set up joint ventures among themselves in order to ensure advantages of scale. BOFA - the waste treatment plant - is such a joint venture project in which all five municipalities participate.

2.4.2. Regulation by laws, plans and standards

Tourism is a highly diverse activity, therefore, several sets of regulations apply. Statutes and regulations of particular importance to tourism and the environment are mentioned below:

- *Planning Act*[40]. The Planning Act includes all levels from the municipal to the national level, defining the division of labour. The role of the national level is to guide and control. However, it is possible for the Government to take initiatives if particular problems or needs make it necessary. This instrument is rarely used. It has, however, been utilized to limit sprawl in coastal zones, which is particularly important in connection with tourism and leisure. The Planning Act gives priority to issues related to the use of space, but requires co-ordination with the plans governing all environmentally related sectors.

  The EU obligation to undertake Environmental Impact Assessments of major developments has been included in the revised Planning Act[41]. The list of

---

40   Lovbekendtgørelse nr 383 af 14.6.1993 om Planlægning

41   Miljø- og Energiministeriets bekendtgørelse nr. 847 af 30. september 1994 om supplerende regler i medfør af Lov om Planlægning

facilities requiring such an assessment prior to their construction includes resorts and hotels larger than 50,000 m². Furthermore, retail centres, infrastructure projects and large landscape changes will need assessment.

During the period this regulation has existed, no full-scale Environmental Impact Assessment procedure has been performed on Bornholm. A less ambitious process was employed in connection with a hotel at Rø, which was solely concerned with possible visual consequences[42].

The County Council is obliged to prepare regional plans which govern the development of housing, retailing and industrial expansion areas, as well as the development of areas for leisure facilities, of infrastructure and supply systems and the development of the countryside. A number of the regulations included in the regional development plan are closely connected to environmental matters. On Bornholm, for instance, this applies to the afforestation plan, the conservation plans and the plan for agricultural development. These plans cater explicitly to the interests of the population and of the tourists when it comes to recreational areas. And they ensure that urbanization will not take place in these areas. In connection with afforestation, a financial incentive programme has been designed to encourage the speeding-up of a process designed to expand forest resources.

The regional plan also covers bicycle trails on the whole of the island. They are meant to benefit tourists and local residents alike.

The regional development plan determines the location of technical facilities, and specifies and co-ordinates initiatives to protect water catchment areas and the marine environments.

Accordingly, the regional development plan is a comprehensive instrument of implementation and control, and the regional plan is detailed even further in supplements published by the county council itself and in the municipal plans, which are supposed to cohere with the objectives and guidelines of the regional development plan.

All five of Bornholm's municipalities have passed local development plans, but some of them have not made any recent revisions, as they have

---

42   As Rø is an environmentally vulnerable location, the lack of a full-scale process has been criticized by Bramsnæs, Annelise and Erik Bølling-Ladegaard: Miljøvurdering. Implementering af VVM i Danmark, Kunstakademiets Arkitektskole, April 1992

developed very slowly over the last decade. Local development plans include almost all the issues covered by the regional development plans, but they describe them in greater detail. In addition, the municipalities set up statutory guidelines applying the use and development of individual properties.

The municipality of Nexø has actively attempted to include tourism in a compressive planning process with a great deal of public participation. The outcome of this planning process was an action plan for the renovation of the summer house areas. In particular, the augmentation of the quality of the houses has been brought into focus, while environmental matters are given a slightly lower priority. The municipality of Rønne has - in compliance with the local development plan - set up extensive conservation guidelines and thrown in financial incentives for the owners of old houses. The conversion of quarries for recreational purposes has also been included in the local development plan.

The local development plans must take into consideration issues dealt with in other plans and they must be co-ordinated with other plans, e.g plans concerning the supply and utility services. Compared to development in the rest of the country, the municipalities of Bornholm have delayed the implementation of, for example, water treatment facilities. Also when it comes to reaction, the local development plans are a fairly "flexible" instrument.

The Planning Act includes a paragraph on the use of summer house areas. Occupation during the off-season period is not allowed except for short breaks and weekends. This also implies that the houses cannot be rented out all year. The environmental consequences are beneficial in the sense that in this way the pressure on natural resources is alleviated. In addition, the supply and utility services have only a limited capacity, and this capacity will usually not be exceeded if the paragraph in the Planning Act is observed.

- *The Nature Conservation Act*[13] aims at the protection of nature with its flora and fauna and their habitats. In addition, this act includes the protection of landscapes, and sites of cultural, scientific and educational interest. Included in the act are instruments to increase the number and scope of such areas and to restore and ensure access to the protected areas.

In the guidelines of to the Act it is mentioned that priority is given to "social"

---

43   Lov nr 9 af 1. marts 1992 om Naturbeskyttelse

objectives, but the need to protect will, in the nature of things, require certain limitations.

The Act protects the following categories of natural resources: lakes, rivers, moors, marshes, littoral meadows, littoral swamps, certain meadows, commons, etc. Normally, changes are not allowed to take place. Regulations applying to the use of the areas also imply that camping and advertising cannot be allowed. Other restrictions may also be imposed. In return, there is generally public access to the protected areas, including cases where the areas are privately owned. The public is instructed to use trails and roads.

In its conservation plan, Bornholm County Council has designated a number of important areas for protection - first and foremost the largest forest district called the "Almindingen" and areas along the coast. Within these areas smaller districts of particular importance have been designated for protection.

Other planning documents are concerned with the use of the natural resources of Bornholm for leisure activities[44]. The preferred mode of regulation is to establish signposted trails: "Many experts consider trails harmful, because the surrounding areas are thought likely to become overrun by too many visitors, who might destroy their qualities. However, the opposite is usually the case. The trails will guide the visitors through the area, and the majority will follow the anticipated routes. Particularly valuable sites can be efficiently protected, areas which might have been injured if trails had formed incidentally" (p 60).

The Nature Conservation Act grants powers to make public purchases of land or to grant loans or subsidies to aid the re-establishment of natural resources, for interpretation, etc. In 1995, as much as DKK 45 million was allocated by Parliament for this purpose. This fund of financial resources from which both private and public organisations may benefit, is regarded as an important supplement when it comes to increasing an area's opportunities of creating leisure and tourism facilities. Over the last few years, Bornholm has enjoyed an inflow of resources for projects concerned with the re-establishment of marshes, stone walls, ponds, woodlands and rivers[45].

---

44   Bornholms Amt: Friluftslivets interesseområder, 1984

45   Miljøministeriet: Naturforvaltning, Årsberetninger and Amtsrådsforeningen: Amterne i naturen, København, 1994

- *Coastal Protection Regulation.* Coastal protection regulations are of immense interest in relation to tourism and leisure. In Danish legislation, coastal protection was previously independently regulated by separate statutes, but has now become part of the Planning Act[46]. The coastal zone has been defined as a strip of land which is three kilometres wide, and where more stringent planning is required and expansion of leisure facilities can only be limited in scale[47].

The intention underlying the coastal regulations is to keep undeveloped coastal countryside free of buildings in the future, and to ensure that existing urbanisation is developed in accordance with the natural environment and landscapes in which they are located. New tourist and leisure developments can only take place if they have been included in a tourist development plan, and if they are located adjacent to existing towns or other resorts. However, these regulations do not make it possible to alter existing legal uses of coastal areas, however objectionable they may seem. A further purpose of these regulations is to improve the coastal areas so as enhance their value as leisure and recreational resources.

In comparison to the rest of Denmark, Bornholm's coastal zone is rather heavily urbanised. Some 50-70 per cent of the south coast is developed as compared to 30-50 per cent of the rest of the island[48]. In its planning instruments, the County Council has estimated that the land reservations made to accommodate camp sites, hotels and apartments, golf courses and marinas, which were already included in previous plans, are sufficient. There will be no further development of summer house areas in the coastal zone, but developments may take place inland.

Public access to the coast is to be ensured.

- *The Environmental Protection Act[49]* regulates the discharges from enterprises and industries. The types of production processes considered particularly offensive are under an obligation to be controlled and approved by the

---

46   Miljøministeriets cirkulære af 19. december 1991: Cirkulære om planlægning og administra-
      tion af kystområder; now included in: Lovbekendtgørelse af 16. august 1994 om planlægning

47   Miljø- og Energiministeriet: Vejledning om planlægning i kystområderne, København 1995

48   Miljøministeriet: Miljøtilstanden i Danmark, København 1991

49   Lov nr. 590 af 27.6.1994 om Miljøbeskyttelse

authorities. Alternatively, these activities may be regulated by joint rules applying to an entire industrial branch and negotiated with the trade organisations.

In regard to tourism, only amusement parks are covered directly by the Environmental Protection Act. The authorities are, however, empowered to handle noise problems caused by other types of leisure activities.

Since the passing of the first environmental legislation in the early 70s, the nature of environmental regulations has changed slightly. From being framework legislation predominantly used in planning activities, the environmental regulations have shifted towards more firmly defined rules and standards, and more specific objectives designed to contain the effect of certain activities on the environment[50]. This development stems mostly from the fact that the pool of knowledge on environmental impacts has been expanded over the years, and it has been recognized that some tightening-up was essential in order to minimize environmental impacts. Moe (1994) mentions the waste water treatment plan, which was successful in imposing very high standards on the municipalities. The same plan introduced measures applying to agriculture, but these did not lead to the environmental benefits envisaged.

2.4.3. Regulation by means of financial instruments

Recent revisions of the Environmental Protection Act introduce new regulation methods. For instance, a greater emphasis is placed on the implementation of cleaner technologies in the industries. These measures are not particularly relevant to most types of tourist enterprises.

However, along with the renewal of statutes and regulations, green taxes have to an increasing extent been introduced as a supplementary instrument in environmental regulation. Tax laws include these measures[51].

For reasons of competitiveness, energy taxes were previously paid predominantly by households rather than enterprises. Enterprises were not encouraged to save quite as much energy, but this principle has now become a matter of change. The Ministry of

---

50   Moe, Mogens: Miljøret - Miljøbeskyttelse, Gad, København, 1994

51   Lovforslag L 209 af 6.4.1995 om ændring af lov om kuldioxid af visse energiprodukter. Lovforslag L 210 om ændring af lov om energiafgift af mineralolieprodukter m.v. og lov om afgift af stenkul, brunkul og koks, og lov om afgift af elektricitet, Lovforslag L. 213 af 6.4.1995 om afgift af svovl.

Finance calculates that hotels and restaurants will have to pay 3.7 per cent of the energy taxes, which corresponds to their share of employment[52]. The cultural and attraction sectors will have to pay 0.7 per cent. These amounts are not trivial for the sectors concerned, and the Bornholm trade organisations have protested against these taxes.

However, the authorities anticipate that the tourism industry will be able to reduce its payment of green taxes by 10-20 per cent by means of introducing saving measures. Part of the taxes will be channelled back into those industries that implement innovative saving measures and cleaner technologies - in the shape of loans and subsidies. The industrial community on Bornholm and elsewhere has still not launched any comprehensive strategies to exploit these types of opportunities.

For the time being, ferry transportation is exempted from green taxes. Nevertheless, BornholmsTrafikken (the ferry company) is at present closely investigating its emissions of fuel waste and comparing it with the financial advantages available upon the introduction of energy-saving measures. This is done by means of a pilot project initiated in co-operation with the Ministry of Energy. But the ferry company has not considered how the issue of future green taxes will affect saving measures in this enterprise or how they might affect the trade as such.

Green taxes, as mentioned above, are paid by the entire Danish nation. Other types of price and market related measures are, however, a matter for local decision. In principle, the price paid for water, waste water treatment, heating and solid waste collection must correspond to the costs of these facilities. These services are not expected to create revenue. The authorities and the semi-public enterprises in charge of providing these services are in general keen to encourage households and enterprises to save energy. Water meters are now being introduced on Bornholm. Businesses with a high energy consumption are offered energy checks by the electricity supplier. Tourism enterprises appreciate this service and queue up for it.

The solid waste treatment plant, BOFA, is paid according to the amount of waste collected and according to the collection frequency. BOFA cannot charge too high a price, as the waste might then be disposed of illegally and left to pollute the countryside. The population can deliver waste directly to the treatment plant without incurring any expenses, a fact which is also to an increasing extent being communicated to tourists.

Over time the authorities and businesses on Bornholm have exploited regional and other types of development schemes and programmes whenever possible, EU-financed as well as schemes financed by the Danish government. Earlier, the island received subsidies

---

52   Finansministeriet: Grønne afgifter og erhvervene, København 1994

for experimental and advanced types of energy supply, for instance solar heating, biomass and wind energy. Especially in the 1980s, the island enjoyed a "demonstration status" in these respects, and still receives delegations from Denmark and abroad.

The existence of subsidies, investment programmes and financial transfers has been and still is of essential importance to the island's economic situation [53]. The EU-financed programmes promote environmental issues in a fairly indirect way. But, for instance in the Interreg and the Borntek programmes, support is only given to enterprises which fulfil environmental requirements[54]. In the Objective 5b programme, FIUF and PESCA[56] subsidies will be given to specific environmental projects.

2.4.4. Collaborative and behavioural measures

As described in the previous sections, legal instruments and planning and financial instruments constitute important modes of environmental regulation in Denmark and on Bornholm. Other instruments are, however, also used to influence the behaviour of tourism enterprises and tourists. Trade activities and codices are measures which will be outlined in this section.

As a result of EU environmental initiatives manufacturing enterprises can participate in voluntary environmental accounting and management schemes[57]. In its guidelines, the Ministry for the Environment opens up a possibility for other industrial sectors to participate. However, no systematic plans have been launched by the tourism industry in response to this regulation. Nevertheless, other parallel initiatives aiming to introduce the tourism industry to environmental management codes have been taken, e.g. Den grønne Nøgle (The Green Key), an eco-label for which hotels and youth hostels can apply. The concept covers such issues as measures to save drinking water, energy

---

53   Schønemann, Steen: En ø uden tilskud. En analyse af betalingerne mellem Bornholm og det øvrige Danmark og et bud på, hvad der sker, hvis den ophører, Bornholms Forskningscenter, 1995

54   Bornholms Amt: Interreg Bornholm, 1992; Jensen, Susanne et al: Borntek. Evaluering af et program for erhvervsudvikling på Bornholm 1988-1992. Institut for grænseregionsforskning, Åbenrå, 1994

55   Financial instrument for fisheries development (EU/Danish national programme)

56   EU programme for the restructuring of the fisheries sector

57   Rådets Forordning (EØF) nr 1836/1993 af 29.6.1993 om industrivirksomheders frivillige deltagelse i fællesskabsforordning for miljøstyring og miljørevision

savings, a codex for laundries, kitchens, gardening, and standards applying to guest information and staff training. After an (annually repeated) approval process, the enterprise in question is allowed to use the logo and marketing support, etc. attached to the concept.

The local branch of the hotel and restaurant association has been particularly active promoting the eco-label among member enterprises, and it has been fairly successful. However, a very large number of hotels and guest houses on the island have not applied for approval, and have not launched other environmental initiatives. The authorities have only done a little to promote the concept on the island, and the local tourist associations concentrate their efforts on marketing, as they find it impossible to cope with matters that are considered the internal affairs of member enterprises.

One single municipality, Nexø, has launched a more comprehensive strategy and action plan. An environmental handbook[58] for camp sites, hotels, youth hostels and restaurants was produced. The handbook is made up of brief and operational check lists and contains a recommendation advising the enterprises to go over these lists. In addition, the municipality has started a dialogue with the owners of summer houses - a highly fragmented group of tourist facility providers. The objective is to ensure the speeding-up of the renovation process in the summer house areas, while environmental issues are given a lower priority.

Bornholm is the only destination in Denmark to have got the preparations for an environmental improvement and (eventual) certification procedure off the ground[59]. This project is a joint initiative supported by many sectors of tourism on the island: tourist associations, trade organisations, authorities, NGOs, etc. The project is based on the voluntary actions of the participants. The underlying philosophy is that self-regulation represents a more attractive and less compromising mode of moving the sector towards a concepts of sustainability in tourism.

It may be concluded that the trade codes and trade activities established have been of limited scale and scope, although there are indications that interest in these matter is rising. Getting individual enterprises to participate in these activities will require considerable effort, as thoroughly prepared local concepts (for instance destination certifications) are still lacking.

---

58   Nexø kommune: Miljøhåndbog for turistvirksomheder i Nexø kommune, n.d.

59   HORECON: Bornholm. En ø med miljøvenlig turisme, n.d.; and HORECON: Afrapportering af forprojekt: "Bornholm - en ø med miljøbevidst turisme", n.d.

In the matter of communicating the behavioural codes to the tourists, the general picture is completely different. Tourists seem to be far more recognized as a target group for environmental information than do businesses. The County Council publishes books and brochures in several languages on many topics and single attractions. A very comprehensive guidebook to scenic attractions with descriptions, photographs and maps is available, but it does not contain a code of conduct to be followed by visitors to the areas[60]. Smaller pamphlets, for instance on specified localities or on selected issues of flora and fauna, and maps of trails are also available. In some cases, for instance in the information material about Paradisbakkerne and Døndalen, the tourists are asked to show consideration and urged:

- not to take away plants and trees
- not to fish in the streams
- to pass with care, if walking away from the trails
- not to litter
- to keep their dog on a leash
- to consider the risks of fire.

In these areas, the visitors will find signboards which also give hints of how to pay attention to the environment. As mentioned earlier, the most vulnerable localities are not shown in brochures or on signboards so as to preserve their qualities.

The County Council publishes brochures for distribution among the users of marinas. There are no codes of conduct for towns, resorts and other tourist districts.

Guided walking tours are offered by the "nature guides", an institution which can be found in all Denmark's counties. The guides are available to anybody who might be interested in the natural resources of Bornholm. As Bornholm is a popular destination for school groups, this service is aimed very much at the younger age groups. Other organizations also offer guided tours of the island. The overall capacity of this type of service is limited, but may be considered very efficient when it comes to influencing behaviour.

Bornholm has some small documentation centres. One centre, Grynebækken, failed to hold on to sufficient means to finance its ambitious exhibitions demonstrating organic waste water treatment, composting, greenhousing, etc. Another initiative has been launched - Natur Bornholm - which is planned to become a major attraction, documenting important aspects of the natural environment of the island. The future

---

60   Samvirkende Bornholmske Turistforeninger and Bornholms Amt: På tur i Bornholms natur, 1989

prospects of Natur Bornholm are not clear at the time of writing.

On the subject of influencing tourists' behaviour, it should finally be mentioned that the tourist association of Nexø has published a local guide pamphlet. This pamphlet includes an outline description of the solid waste treatment system. The reason for this initiative may be found in many enquiries made by tourists to the tourist office concerning the waste collection system.

2.4.5. Conclusions on environmental regulatory instruments

The above outline description of the environmental regulations concerned with tourism in Denmark and on Bornholm reveals the following:

- Profound planning traditions have created a firm basic knowledge of the location of environmentally vulnerable sites and the extent of environmentally harmful activities and discharges. Over the years protection zones have been established, and a stabilisation of environmental constraints has taken place. In the course of the last decade it has been considered necessary to launch measures to increase the reserves of natural assets and to improve the environmental state of the art in general. Bornholm was an early starter when it came to recycling and renewable energies, but at present the island can no longer be claimed to be in the forefront of developments.

- The use of green taxes and other financial instruments and market philo-sophies as part of environmental policies has been strengthened. The taxation laws of 1994 introduce the most powerful instruments ever seen, aimed at motivating industries to take serious action. Also local financial measures, such as water metering, have been expanded over the past few years.

- Regulation of behaviour is predominantly directed towards tourists rather than tourism enterprises. A range of publications and other types of documentation efforts are supported by the County Council. Collaborative and voluntary efforts initiated by the trade associations can be found, but progress is still rather slow.

As can be seen from this analysis, environmental regulation in tourism is a complex matter and consists of measures and philosophies originating from several regulatory traditions. But it is very clear that some planning and legal instruments, which have formed the basis of Danish environmental policies for more than two decades, are still extremely important. In the planning process, documentation has also been the source for devising supplementary interpretative instruments. Green taxes have recently been introduced at the national level, but the application of financial instruments at the local level is still to come.

In comparison to the public initiatives, the tourism industry lags far behind. The trade associations do participate in joint initiatives with the public sector, but there is still a lack of comprehensive objectives and no general adoption of specific objectives or codes of conduct can be seen. The industry is not a forceful supporter of the idea of introducing environmental strategies on the islands - either formally or informally. A trade-based environmental lobby does not exist. Accordingly, the tourism industry seems to let the public sector play the pioneering role.

In order to explain the low awareness in regard to environmental strategies and initiatives in the tourism sector, one should take the following into consideration:

- Environmental problems are not regarded as being key problems of the island. Public authorities and the tourism industry tend to share this understanding. Very visible problems such as the handling of solid waste in the summer house areas and the algae on the beaches are exceptions to this rule. Less visible and potential constraints (for instance in connection with the supply of drinking water) receive less attention. A proactive policy is delayed.

- The local understanding is that environmental regulations are imposed from "above" and from the "outside", e.g. from the Government, and then channelled through regional and local planning systems. The scope for joint local action is still limited. Experience gained via the eco-labelling initiative and via the preparations for a "green destination concept" does, however, broaden people's understanding and cause them to see that environmental actions could benefit the local tourism industry.

- Neither the tourism industry nor the authorities have made any thorough investigation into the question of whether tourists would appreciate it if Bornholm had a clearer environmental profile. With the exception of a few areas, with which tourists tend to express dissatisfaction, the local tourism industry does not know whether or how a clearer profile and strategy might create new market opportunities.

The environment is still only emerging as an issue on Bornholm, the main reason being that environmental problems are not imminently impending.

2.5. Environmental innovations

In this section a number of projects and initiatives within the field of tourism and the environment will be spotlighted. Whether environmental regulations are responsible or partly responsible for bringing about innovation will be given particular emphasis in this analysis.

2.5.1. Bicycle trails

In 1995, nearly 200 kilometres of bicycle trails were available to cyclists on Bornholm. They were established on closed-down railway lines, along minor, less busy roads, and new tracks were built for this specific purpose. Bornholm was the first place in Denmark to undertake a co-ordinated and county-wide planning of cycling routes.

The objective of establishing these trails was to supply tourists and residents with a system of trails with a high level of utilities. At the same time, the trails were to lead past attractive natural assets and cultural facilities. Any favourable impacts on the environment arising out of the reduction of emissions from other modes of transportation received far less attention.

The idea of establishing a co-ordinated bicycle trail system was integrated into the planning philosophies of the late 1970s. The county development plan was found to be an efficient means of regulation in regard to this type of infrastructure which involved the crossing of private property and municipal property boundaries.

At the time when it was established, a co-ordinated and sign-posted network of bicycle trails represented an innovation in its own respect. Bornholm became a source of inspiration to other county councils in Denmark. The activities on the island of Bornholm resulted in the initiation of closer co-operative relations between the authorities and organisations such as the "Bicycling Association". Along with the county council and local tourist offices, the bicycling association has been very active marketing the trail systems to its members and non-members. Thus trail systems gradually became institutionalised.

This innovative initiative has not stopped at the provision of the new infrastructure and the marketing of it. Private entrepreneurs have broadened the concept. All over the island it has become possible to rent bicycles. Along the routes catering establishments and retail shops have been established. Specialised travel agencies offer package tours which include ferry transportation, bicycle hire and accommodation.

In the case of the bicycle routes, the authorities must be said to have inaugurated a long-term policy which has - over the years - been followed up by many incremental innovations initiated by private entrepreneurs.

2.5.2. Eco-hotel

As a result of the eco-labelling campaign, which was aimed at hotels, the idea of creating an eco-hotel arose. The initiators were some of the active members of the local hotel and restaurant association and also came from the tourism consulting enterprise of HORECON, which is based in Copenhagen.

An eco-hotel was supposed to fulfil environmental requirements which are considerably stricter than the ones required of "Green Key" hotels. This hotel was planned to be built from local and recyclable materials; all types of energy saving and recycling methods were to be introduced.

In these respects, the hotel complied with the philosophy carried into effect in many eco-lodging projects all over the world. But in one respect the eco-hotel was planned to go beyond established ideas. In co-operation with "Baltic Educational Project" the educational department of the hotel was to be involved in the training of Polish and Baltic environmentalists and civil servants.

In regard to the vacational market, a co-operation effort involving the visitor attraction of Natur Bornholm was supposed to be of mutual benefit. Furthermore, the hotel was to ensure that families with children could be offered activities in organic agriculture.

In the course of 1995 a feasibility study was performed and the initiators made attempts to raise capital for the project. As competition in the hotel trade is fierce and excess capacity is an established fact, the initiators were forced to put off the project until a later time.

2.5.3. Public coach tours

Public bus transport on Bornholm is co-ordinated by Bornholms Amts Trafikselskab (BAT). BAT does not own the buses but operates through private contractors and DSB, the Danish state railway company. Public transport is predominantly regarded as a service offered to residents, and from an environmental point of view public transport is usually a better solution than private cars.

Over the last few years, BAT has offered coach tours to tourists during the summer.

"The Green Bus" takes its passengers to see the solid waste treatment plant, organic agricultural holdings, wildlife reserves and nature regeneration projects. On these tours, a guide travels with the tourists on the bus. Other types of tours visit conventional agricultural holdings and arts and crafts workshops.

BAT also attempts to appeal to tourists to take ordinary buses to attractions and nature reserves. A pamphlet explaining the possibilities is published.

What is so special about the services provided by the BAT company is that the company is actively cultivating co-operative relations with many types of attractions. Attractions which do not normally form part of the tourism product have gained an opportunity to expose themselves to tourists.

The BAT case illustrates that innovations may successfully be undertaken within the field of "logistics". In this case, modifications to the transportation system have enhanced the opportunities for other environmentally interesting projects and activities.

2.5.4. Solar energy in the Brændesgårdshaven amusement park

Brændesgårdshaven is an amusement park with water switchbacks, etc. In order to ensure a sufficient comfort level, the water has to be heated.

In 1991, the park invested in a 180 m^2 solar energy system, sufficient to ensure a high enough heating level on sunny days. In cloudy weather, the central heating system is used as an auxiliary system.

The investment was prompted by the existence of a governmental investment subsidy scheme, reducing the price by 30 per cent and thus enabling the project to be realized in full. Green taxes will enhance the financial benefits.

Brændesgårdshaven discovered that solar energy meets with positive comments from tourists, and the management decided to include environmental arguments in its marketing material.

This case illustrates the fact that financial calculations are of major importance to individual enterprises. Usually Bornholm businesses are not to be found among the "prime movers" when it comes to new technology and environmental investments. Brændesgårdshaven did, however, discover the marketing benefits of fast action. Later imitators will probably not be able to harvest this type of benefit.

2.5.5. Clean beach - active beach

The municipality of Nexø and the Nexø-Dueodde Tourist Association engage in a job training scheme involving a number of unemployed people. They have a dual task: keeping the beaches free of refuse and algae. But they also offer other types of services to guests visiting the beaches, e.g. guidance concerning the flora and fauna in the district, and they organize beach work-out programmes, competitions for children, etc.

The jobs of the service staff reflect the actual needs that must be met on the beaches. But as part of a training scheme, it has been equally important to ensure that the unemployed trainees gain a set of qualifications which might be useful in relation to other types of jobs, for instance service mindedness, work flexibility, insight into the natural environment, operation and maintenance of machinery, language skills, etc.

The scheme is supported by the EU's Social Fund. Without this type of finance this activity would probably not have been established.

2.5.6. The Green Key

A number of hotels on Bornholm have been certified and allowed to carry the symbol of the "Green Key". The following criteria are included in the compulsory section of the concept:

Guest information
Staff information
Water:
>   Water meters
>   Low volume WC cisterns
>   No dripping taps or leaky cisterns
>   Water saving devices on taps
>   One-hand mixers
>   "Dead man's handle" in kitchens
>   Appropriate temperature in swimming pools
>   Low volume flush systems in urinals

Washing and cleaning
>   Change of towels on guests' request
>   Dosage of cleaning agents and detergents according to documentation

Waste
>   Separation into six fragments
>   Co-operation with the local waste handler
>   Storing of waste in containers approved by the authorities

Food waste disposal units that require running water are not to be used

No disposable cups, etc. For special events, degradable cups, etc. allowed

Limited use of foodstuffs in individual wrappings

Energy

Energy management programme to be introduced

Consulting services to be acquired to adjust larger consumers of energy

Optimization of the outdoor lighting

Correct temperatures in refrigerating and freezing appliances

Intact sealing strips in refrigerators and freezers

Grease separators must be cleaned weekly

Heat regulation systems in each room

Optimal boiling/frying equipment

Covered water baths in kitchens

Cookers, electricity and gas to be switched off when not required

Food

Selection of organic food in breakfast menus

Plan for increased use of organic foods

Low-fat menu available

Indoor climate

Airing of rooms on departure

Smoke-free department in restaurant

Smoke-free hotel rooms

Outdoor areas

Lawn-mowers electrically-powered or run on unleaded petrol.

A large number of these requirements will combine environmental benefits with financial benefits for the owners of the hotels. After introduction and diffusion to a larger number of hotels, these measures can no longer be regarded as particularly innovative.

2.6. Conclusions

Bornholm's tourism industry cannot be claimed to be particularly innovative in response to environmental constraints and regulations. However, a few initiatives deserve to be singled out. For instance the eco-hotel, which may - if it is ever established - become a demonstration project.

In Denmark, innovations most often take place as part of or in conjunction with activities launched by the public sector. Sometimes an initiative that will benefit tourism will also be of advantage to residents. These facilities are not only the result of environmental regulations but also form an integral part of the philosophy underlying planning and interpretation. Planning has been and still is an important basis from which innovative activities can take off, particularly if the powers to implement the plans are also present.

Private tourism enterprises are reluctant when it comes to the evaluation of long-term market developments or changes in public regulations. But they are alert when the prices charged for water, energy, waste disposal, etc. are increased. However, they utilize standard solutions which will create only short-term benefits. Although exceptions can be found, they will rarely launch into experiments in these matters.

Over the last few years a greater enthusiasm has been observable within the tourism industries. It can, however, primarily be put down to immitative behaviour, and it runs parallel to the introduction of green taxes.

What is the reason for the low business innovativeness in relation to the environment?

First and foremost, there is an understanding that the environment is not a very urgent problem. The carrying capacity of the island is still higher than the constraints envisaged - in the short term economic potential is not threatened. Therefore, environmental issues are only discussed in principle. The long-term opportunities and constraints of importance to the private and public sectors are still only vaguely stated.

Second, it is a well-known fact that tourists visiting Bornholm appreciate the natural environment. At the same time they still do not show any particular preference for the most environmentally friendly products within accommodation, catering, transport, etc. It is important to note that tourists visiting Bornholm are individual consumers, who make up their own product by selecting single elements from the transportation system, hotels, restaurants, attractions and other sources of supply. Package tours to this particular destination are rarely found. This implies that the consumers are *not* organized, they have no environmental lobby to act on their behalf. Not even "wholesalers" (tour operators, or travel agents) are representing the interests of the consumers on Bornholm. Enterprises such as the dominant ferry company and the summer house intermediaries are not particularly aware of their role as representatives of the consumers. In consequence the tourism industry is not met with imperatives from the consumers.

Third, the composition of environmental measures favours particular types of innovations. Planning forms an essential part of the entire range of regulatory efforts, and this planning process often leads to the initiative being taken by the public sector. It should, however, not be forgotten that public initiatives within the fields of energy planning, water supply, conservation of nature and landscapes and the provision of infrastructure have been of essential importance in limiting the environmental constraints existing on the island. Furthermore, tourism is not one of those industrial sectors characterised by discharges that are subjected to particularly keen environmental controls.

Over the last few years a shift towards using market related instruments has been taking place in Danish environmental policies. It can be observed that green taxes have an immediate impact on the behaviour of businesses. Nevertheless, the financial instruments used are aimed primarily at reducing consumption and are implemented in the shape of a tax. Instruments such as subsidies, loans, guarantees, etc. which might further promote sustainable investments, can rarely be obtained by tourism enterprises. The re-channelling of (a part of) the taxes into the enterprises is not organised by the trade itself.

The authorities and businesses on Bornholm have long traditions of exploiting the subsidies systems whenever possible. It is very probable that a similar alertness would be demonstrated if subsidies for environmental initiatives in tourism were available. Such subsidies might - if allocated for this purpose - enhance local innovations.

Tourism enterprises on Bornholm are individualistic. A number of formalized tourism associations, employers' organisations and other types of co-operative bodies exist. But they have to overcome many difficulties when it comes to getting their members to agree on common goals and actions. The most professional tourist enterprises tend to prefer co-operating with enterprises located in other parts of Denmark. Business power is diffuse and does not concentrate in organisational "clans". No joint initiatives based solely on business power are found.

This vacuum leaves room for more initiatives from the county council, the municipalities and some leisure organisations.

3. Mallorca

3.1. Introduction

This case study is concerned with sustainable tourism development within a Southern European framework. The island of Mallorca was chosen as the location for the study.

As in the previous chapter, the case study will also put a particular emphasis on the regulatory aspects of the development towards sustainable tourism. The term regulation has been given a broad interpretation including - of course - environmental legislation and planning initiatives, but also voluntary actions launched by the tourism industry (or other partners having connections with tourism) in order to set up standards of environmental behaviour.

In addition, the occurrence or non-occurrence of innovative actions initiated as a result of regulations will be described and analysed.

Section 3.2 of this chapter will briefly introduce the reader to the state of the art of tourism on Mallorca, while section 3.3 is devoted to a description of the particular environmental problems which the island is facing. An overview of the regulatory system will be given in section 3.4, and finally in section 3.5 some examples of business innovations which have come about in consequence of environmental regulations on Mallorca are presented.

Conclusions and the future perspectives of the regulatory and innovative issues mentioned here will be further commented upon in chapter 5, where comparisons between the three island regions are made.

3.2. The importance of tourism to the island

Mallorca is located in the Western Mediterranean, and it is the largest island in the group of islands called the Balearic Islands. A distance of 180 kilometres separates Mallorca from Barcelona, the location most often referred to as the mainland "anchoring" point.

Mallorca has a surface area of about 3,640 square kilometres and a population of 613,000 of whom 325,000 live in Palma de Mallorca (1994). The number of permanent residents went up by 2.4 per cent between 1986 and 1991. For comparison it might be mentioned that in the same period the population growth in Spain amounted to 0.8 per cent.

Mallorca was one of the very first destinations to receive the benefits of mass tourism. Figure 3.1. shows the development of tourist arrivals since 1960 for Spain and the Balearic Islands. Mallorca is the main tourist destination among the Balearic Islands, accounting for 75 per cent of arrivals (1993).

Tourist arrivals to the Balearic Islands gradually increased, also during the 80s. The last few years are no exception. Especially 1994 will go down as a historic record year in regard to the number of arrivals: 8.2 million.

Figure 3.1. Index of tourist arrivals, Balearic Islands and Spain (foreigners only), 1960-1994, 1983=100

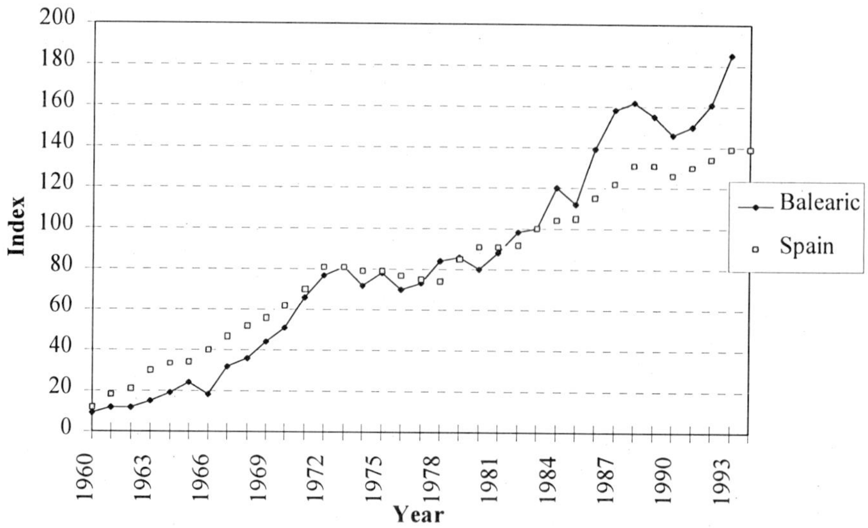

Sources: Ministerio de Comercio y Turismo: Situacion actual del turismo en las Islas Baleares, unpublished report, n.d.; Anuario de Estadísticas de Turismo de España, 1993

Since 1960, the number of tourist arrivals to the Balearic Islands rose by a multiple of 20 - from 400,000 arrivals to over eight million. This development has been gradual. From 1989 to 1993 stagnation set in, but in 1994 the number of arrivals rose again.

In 1993 the total number of tourist arrivals to Mallorca was 5,312 million, representing a growth of six per cent compared with the previous year. The average

60

length of stay is 10 days [61], which corresponds to a total of more than 50 million bednights per year. It is no exaggeration to regard Mallorca as the prototype of the mass tourism destination. Further documentation provided below will underline the characteristics of this mode of tourism.

Table 3.1. The means of transportation, percentage of arrivals

By charter airlines	93
By regular airlines	6
Other means of transportation	1
Total	100

Source: Govern Balear: La despesa turistica, 1993

The table reveals the very nature of tourism: highly organised trips, most of them packaged tours. It is also evident that almost no other means of transportation are used than air transport, although some passengers are transported by ferry from the mainland to Mallorca and between the other Balearic Islands and Mallorca. Certainly Mallorca is a cruise ship destination, but this activity only accounts for a very small proportion of tourist arrivals (probably in the neighbourhood of 100,000 out of 5.3 million).

Throughout the entire development period of Mallorcan tourism, the tour operators have played a decisive role. Without their organizational intervention and marketing capacities, tourism on this island would hardly have been likely to have expanded as it did. The influence of some dominant tour operators can be illustrated as follows: three British tour operators control 80 per cent of the traffic from the UK to the Balearic Islands, representing a total of 32 per cent of all arrivals to the islands[62].

Accordingly, the tour operators have an excessively strong bargaining power vis-à-vis the local industry, and development is heavily dependent on their requirements and allocations.

---

61   David Bruce: Walled Towns, n.d.

62   Govern Balear: Pla Estratègic de Competitivitat de las Islas Baleares. Tom 1: Diagnòstic, 1994, p 35

Table 3.2. Composition of tourist arrivals to the Balearic Islands (by air), by nationality, 1993

	Number of arrivals 1993, thousands	Share in 1979 (all Balearics)	Share in 1994 (all Balearics)
German	2,231	32%	35%
British	2,262	33%	33%
Spanish	887	13%	10%
French	304	5%	4%
Nordic	249	4%	3%
Others	947	13%	15%
Total	8,880	100%	100%

Source: Govern Balear: La despesa turistica, 1993 and Anuario de Estadisticas de Turismo de Espana, 1994

The major markets of the Balearic tourism product can clearly be seen to be the British and German markets, and in particular the German segment has increased in importance in comparison with other nationalities. Since the mid-1970s especially the Nordic and Dutch tourists seem to have preferred other destinations. Selstad[63] shows that with Nordic vacationers one has seen a shift of interest towards the Eastern Mediterranean, partially because of the strong competitiveness of the expanding Turkish tourism industry, partially the result of the tourists' urge to seek new experiences.

The following documentation adds to the picture of the particular characteristics of Mallorcan tourism:

Table 3.3. Modes of accommodation by season, percentage, 1993

	Main season	Mid season	Low season
Hotels	58	61	66
Apartments	37	35	30
Friends and relatives	3	2	3
Other establishments	2	2	1

Source: Govern Balear: La despesa turistica, 1993

Traditional hotel accommodation accounts for the majority of bednights, particularly

---

63   Selstad, Tor: Det nordiske reiselivet i Europa, Oppland Distriktshøgskole, September 1992

(but not very distinctly so) in the low season. The strong emphasis on conventional hotels will, of course, attract certain types of customers, while others - for instance families with small children - may find bungalows or apartments more attractive or appropriate. However, the low preference for self-catering should be related to the price level of restaurant meals - a level which is favourable compared to that of the home countries of the tourists. In this respect Mallorca still has a competitive edge. A survey showed that a total of 40 per cent of tourists cited the price level as one dominant factor motivating their choice of the Balearic Islands for a holiday destination[64].

The local tourism industry and the authorities are particularly concerned by seasonal fluctuations:

Figure 3.2. Seasonal fluctuations, 1991

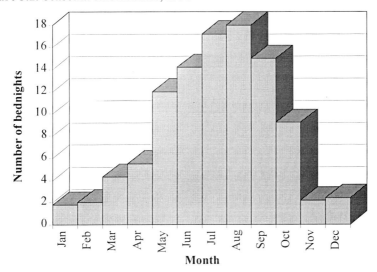

Source: Govern Balear: Pla estratègic de competitivitat de las Islas Baleares, Tom 1: Diagnòstic, 1994, p 41

In spite of the fact that the climate is favourable in all seasons, there is a heavy concentration in the summer months: 84 per cent of tourist arrivals take place between May and October. The result is a considerable excess capacity in the accommodation

---

64   Govern Balear: La despesa turística, 1993

sector. On average, occupancy rates are only 48 per cent[65], based on the number of beds in 1993.

The increase in hotel capacity which has occurred in recent years has added to the problem. From 1985 to 1991, the number of beds was expanded by nearly 30 per cent up to a total of 450,000 beds, but during the same period arrivals showed no sign of a similar growth.

Most of the accommodation capacity (450 hotels) was constructed in the period from 1966-1974. Now, many of these hotels and apartment complexes are in great need of modernisation and upgrading. Refurbishments to bring them up to modern and competitive standards are difficult, partly because of the construction methods (small rooms, high-rise), but more importantly because these areas are densely built up. Supplementary gardens and outdoor facilities cannot easily be established because of the shortage of land and the high prices. Such facilities are considered essential for modern hotels.

The massive inflow of tourists to Mallorca has had a decisive impact on the economy of the island. More than half (58 per cent) of its GNP comes from activities related to tourism, 20 per cent is directly and 22 per cent indirectly related to tourism; 16 per cent is induced incomes[66]. Per capita incomes are 35 per cent higher than in Spain as a whole; Mallorcans earn only 15 per cent less than the average of the entire European Union[67].

Sectors other than the service sector account for a very small share of the Mallorcan economy. Most - e.g. more than 90 per cent - of manufactured products come from the mainland; surprisingly so also do such products as wine and seafood. Agriculture has been declining since tourism has been able to offer better job opportunities.

Construction is mentioned as an important sector which benefited and expanded during tourism's growth period. At present the construction industry is not well enough geared up to be able to enter the growing refurbishment and renovation markets.

Compared with European standards, Mallorcan unemployment figures are high - 13 per

---

65   Govern Balear: Pla Estratègic de Competitivitat de las Islas Baleares, Tom 1: Diagnòstic, 1994

66   Ministerio de Comercio y Turismo: Situacion actual del turismo en las Islas Balear, n.d.

67   IFTO: Planning for sustainable tourism. The Ecomost project, Lewes, UK, n.d.

cent on average - but by Spanish standards this rate is satisfactory. During the off-season unemployment rises to a level of 16 per cent. The reason why it is not higher can be found in the fact that temporary workers leave after the season.

It follows from these facts that, without any doubt, tourism is the most important industry on Mallorca. The local government and the Regional Tourist Board are fully aware of the benefits of tourism. The situation is, however, by no means considered satisfactory, and the authorities and the tourism industry place particular emphasis on the seasonal fluctuations which are described as a problem - and a challenge for the future.

Although it is envisaged that tourism will never stop playing an important role, the regional government has launched initiatives which aim at a diversification of economic activities. "The strategic development plan - the Balearic Islands innovative region" includes the creation of the "Balearic Innovation Park" in connection with the university. This park is designed to encourage the development and implementation of new technologies and telecommunication opportunities[68]. In 1995 this plan was in its initial stages. Though the activities of the park will probably also support and enhance the professionalization of tourism, the main objective is to encourage other types of activities in the sphere of "high-tech, high-skill", etc.

To conclude, Mallorca is a very important tourist destination. Businesses and the authorities are very much aware of the blessings and the pitfalls of this dependency. The necessity to shift gear and to launch innovative measures in order to ensure future competitive advantages are themes in the forefront of political discussions.

From an environmental point of view the characteristics of Mallorcan tourism result in the following observations:

- The number of tourists alone (5.5 million arrivals per year (1995)) may be considered a stress factor in itself, particularly when related to the limited water supply and infrastructural capacities. Authorities as well as environmental organizations seem to agree that the capacities of the island have already been exceeded.

- The way Mallorcan tourism is structured does, however, give rise to some reservations to this general conclusion. Tourists are concentrated within a

---

68   Govern Balear: The Balearic Innovative Region, 1992, and Govern Balear: Pla Estratègic de Competitivitat de las Islas Baleares, Tom 2, Propostes, 1994

few areas, which therefore have a very high density. In terms of environmental measures, the higher densities may be considered more manageable than the opposite situation, with tourists being dispersed over a large area. But the high densities are no good when it comes to future market demand.

• Another characteristic of charter tourism is the fact that tour operators handle the transfer of tourists by means of buses, thus limiting the pressure on the roads. This fact also tends to reduce people's inclination to use private cars and taxis for transportation. Having arrived in Mallorca, people do not move around a lot.

• A large proportion of the tourists are Germans who to an increasing extent express concern for the environment. Surveys on Mallorca confirm that this important tourism market gives higher priority to environmental matters than any other marke[69]. The surveys also show that environmental awareness among all tourists to the Balearic Islands is increasing with considerable speed, and the issue has reached a level of concern where it cannot be ignored.

3.3. The nature and extent of environmental constraints

Tourism affects the environment - primarily, but not exclusively - in a negative way. At the same time tourists and the tourism industry will have less than optimum conditions if the environment is degraded. This section identifies the particular environmental problems of Mallorca. The sources of this analysis are official registrations of the present state of affairs and interviews with key persons. Supplementary documentation was collected through tourist surveys indicating the tourists' opinion of environmental conditions on the island - as well as through other studies.

This information will be compared to data on vulnerability, when such data are available.

The following themes will be covered in the analysis:

• Changes in landscapes and towns

---

69   Govern Balear: La despesa turística, 1993

- Fresh water supply
- Waste water treatment
- Noise
- Solid waste treatment
- Energy supply.

3.3.1. Changes in landscapes and towns

Beaches and coastline. One of the most obvious impacts of mass tourism can easily be observed on Mallorca. Kilometres of the most beautiful coastline have been spoiled by massive construction activities. This development has taken place in recent years, i.e. since the beginning of the 1960s. The municipalities where these developments are located are not able to give any exact indication of the density of the areas built up in this way, but generally the hotels constructed are high-rise (6-18 floors), though in recent years designs with a lower number of floors seem to have been preferred by the developers. The intensive exploitation of land resources means that the space available for gardens, parks, promenades, sports facilities, etc. is scarce. In many cases, beaches are overhung by hotel terraces, etc., although access to Spanish beaches is always public.

Some early hotels were constructed directly on the beach, so that other hotel guests' access to the sea is now blocked, i.e. guests of those hotels which are situated further away from the seafront.

There are still, however, unused planning permissions in the tourist districts, facilitating a considerable growth in the capacity of hotels and apartments. The authorities have not calculated the spare capacity - a capacity which is in any case a subject of continual change, as building conditions are being negotiated and bargained over.

The high density is concentrated in the zones that lie within walking distance of the beach. Behind this zone the land is used extensively, and agricultural utilization takes over. Accordingly, there are usually no intermediary zones separating the high-rise areas and the hinterland.

The heavy concentration of tourist facilities in the Palma Bay and the Alcudia Bay imply that other parts - the majority - of the coastline is less influenced by organized tourism. These areas include valuable natural resources and beautyspots. A considerable part of these resources is protected by law (see below).

The growth of the tourism industry led to migration from the agricultural districts of Mallorca to the better paid and more prestigious jobs in the towns and holiday resorts. Market forces also put agricultural production under pressure, resulting in neglect and in many cases erosion of the traditional landscapes. The decline of agriculture has led to the present situation where large amounts of food products are being imported to the island from the mainland.

Some sports activities are performed in the abandoned areas, for instance "jeep safaris". Although still limited in scale, if developed, this activity would add to the problems of erosion and degradation, particularly of sand dunes[70].

Towns. Mallorca has a considerable number of ancient monuments. The city of Palma, and smaller towns such as Alcudia, have Roman or Medieval origins, and they are well preserved. The awareness of the value of these resources has grown in recent years. The Mallorcan population recognizes its important heritage. In addition, the architectural heritage is increasingly included in marketing efforts directed at tourists.

Alcudia is a member of the international organization "Walled Towns", an organization aiming to increase awareness of the qualities of medieval townscapes and to promote protection and restoration efforts. Sustainability is a distinct issue in these endeavours[71].

Natural resources. The Regional Government recently approved a bill which will protect more than one third of its territory as natural areas of special interest. These areas include mountains, coastlines, marshes and areas of particular interest because of their flora or fauna[72].

The archipelago of Cabrera, which is located immediately south of Mallorca, is a national park where special restrictions protect the natural environment from human interference. The wetlands of S'Albufera have also been turned into a natural park. Other natural parks are Cala Mondrago (beaches) and Dragonera (south west island).

---

70   Coll Perello, Margarita: Turismo y medio ambiente: Hacia un turismo compatible, student dissertation, Universitat de las Islas Baleares, n.d.

71   David Bruce: A Handbook of Good Practice for Sustainable Tourism in Walled Towns, Bristol Business School, October 1993

72   IBATUR: Espais Naturals de les Illes Balear, 1992 and Govern Balear: Gesetz über Naturlandschaften gemäss städtebaulichen Regelungen für besonders geschützte Zonen der Balearen, pamphlet

Of the nearly 1,400 square kilometres of protected area, only 100 square kilometres is publicly owned land. All protected areas are accessible, as roads or tracks for cars, bicycles or pedestrians can normally be used. In reality and in many cases, however, permission to enter must be obtained from the owners of the property.

These access restrictions, enforced as a consequence of the right to privacy, limit the opportunities of tourists with a particular interest in the natural environment to smaller areas and public roads. The sense of private property is strongly developed on Mallorca, and interference with property rights is seldom tolerated. It is said that foreign residents are even less inclined to allow people onto their land.

The restricted possibilities for gaining access to natural resources result in a fairly efficient protection of the most vulnerable areas. Protection against forest fires is as essential as environmental protection. But the opportunities for tourists to take "special interest holidays" in nature seem to be very few, even in areas which cannot be considered vulnerable.

So far the access restrictions have not proven critical. Crowding and conflicts over the use of natural resources have only been reported in a very few places and instances. Silence this matter is primarily because a large majority of vacationers favour other activities than those which are naturebased. Travel and tourism organizations are now becoming aware of the needs of special interest groups, though no policies to accommodate advance requirements have as yet been articulated.

3.3.2. Fresh water supply

The supply of fresh water is a critical factor determining the development of tourism on Mallorca. Mallorca is short of water. Over a number of years, rainfall has been less than sufficient to ensure the recharging of reserves.

The shortage of water has been so serious that the island has needed emergency supplies shipped in from the mainland by tankers. The expansion of tourism is one, but not the single, cause of the water shortage. However, an increase in the tourists' and the local population's consumption of water might prove disastrous[73]. Ordinarily, a country-dwelling Mallorcan would not use more than 140 litres per day, a city-dweller uses 250 litres and the average tourist 440 litres. A luxury tourist may use up

---

73   Ashdown Environmental Limited.: Water supply and sewage disposal specialist study, 1993, refered to by IFTO: Planning for sustainable tourism. The ECOMOST project, n.d.

to 800 litres a day, according to Boers and Bosch[74].

The golf courses form a crucial element in the discussion of water consumption. Plans to expand the number of courses from 15 to 20 are in hand, but the use of water to keep the green image intact is enormous. Whether permission to build new golf courses is given will, however, depend on the possibilities of obtaining semi-purified water from the urban areas. For the following reasons, this may still not fully solve the environmental constraints:

The demand for water has already had serious irreversible environmental impacts. The aquifers (subterranean water-storing deposits or rocks) are not fully recharged, resulting in a significant lowering of the ground water table. Mallorca depends on its ground water. The inflow of sea water into the fresh water deposits causes salt contamination, which in turn necessitates expensive treatment. The ground water quality is further compromised because of the presence of high chloride and nitrate concentrations. In some areas treatment plants will be needed if EC standards are to be met, which will probably double the price of water[75].

In addition, desalination plants have been considered for the city of Palma and its surroundings. Yet this is an even more expensive solution estimated to increase the price of water around 10 times.

Tourists cannot be expected to be fully aware of the serious water problems, as they are not systematically informed by tour operators, authorities or hotels. Only 10 per cent of tourists on Mallorca realized that there was a water shortage. Nevertheless, a considerable recognition and acceptance of the measures designed to alleviate the pressure on this resource can be found among tourists. The table shows the result of a survey containing inquiries on water saving measures:

---

74   Boers, H. and M. Bosh: The earth as a holiday resort. An introduction to tourism and the environment, Utrecht, 1994

75   IFTO: Planning for sustainable tourism. The ECOMOST project, Lewes, n.d.

Table 3.4. Reduction of water consumption considered sensible, percentage of answers

Nationality	Summer	Winter
German speaking countries	35	52
Great Britain	16	28
Spain	11	42
Others	36	42

Source: IFTO: Planning for sustainable development. The ECOMOST project, n.a.

The willingness to consider such measures "sensible" is strongest among German speaking tourists and "others" (Nordic, Dutch, French, Italians, etc.). However, in the summer, tourists are generally less inclined to save water, either because water is more needed for showers, etc., or because the tourist segments differ.

3.3.3. Waste water treatment

The beaches on Mallorca are considered clean, and a considerable emphasis is placed on efforts to keep the beaches and the bathing water free of pollution from chemicals and solid substances. The Municipality of Calvia, for instance, considers acquiring the Blue Flag essential. Altogether the Balearic Isles were given 55 Blue Flags in 1994.

Limited amounts (one third) of municipal waste water is led directly into the sea after treatment. Most of the water is recycled for use in agriculture, gardens and on golf courses, and to re-establish ground water reserves, and this practice will be further expanded. Limited amounts of industrial waste water are discharged into the marine environment since manufacturing industries are of minor importance to the island. The same can be said about agriculture, which means that run-offs containing nutrients causing eutrophication and associated problems only occur to a limited extent.

Mallorca is, however, a part of the larger Mediterranean eco-system. "Environmental degradation in the Mediterranean Basin has reached serious levels in recent years and is likely to worsen"[76]. According to the World Bank investigations, Mallorca is not among the ecologically most sensitive areas in the Mediterranean, but conflicts over the use of resources could occur here in the future. Tourism is likely to be negatively influenced by pollution caused by coastal urban centres in Spain, France and Italy - in

---

76   The World Bank and The European Investment Bank: The Environmental Program for the Mediterranean. Preserving a Shared Heritage and Managing a Common Resource, Luxembourg, 1990, p. 17

spite of the fact that these countries are mounting programmes to meet EU effluent and emission standards[77].

New and improved sewage treatments plants are at present being erected to ensure that European standards can be met. The standard of much private equipment in hotels, etc. is questionable. It is common for households to have septic tanks[78]. There is still some way to go.

3.3.4. Noise

The noise reported on Mallorca is mostly caused by the tourists themselves, rather than by industrial activities. The population density of the touristic zones causes noise problems which are aggravated even more by numerous animation and entertainment activities, many bars and discotheques, etc. Furthermore, traffic planning has been insufficient, causing many accommodation facilities to suffer from traffic noise.

Conflicts between tourists wanting quietness and tourists participating in (nightly) entertainment activities are so often experienced that certain municipalities are considering a more distinct zoning in new developments, and better traffic separation. Tour operators also attempt to handle the problems before they result in complaints by "segmenting" hotels and customers into "noisy" and "quiet" groups.

3.3.5. Solid waste treatment

Tourism - and the fairly wealthy local population - generates considerable and growing volumes of solid waste. "It has been calculated that a tourist produces 50 per cent more rubbish than a Mallorcan resident. The chairman of the Playa del Palma hoteliers' organization has described how the total waste production of his hotel rose by 30 per cent in just four years. Rubbish left behind in the hotel bedrooms had risen by 50 per cent".[79] The public debate has now for some time been focusing on the problems

---

77   Ibid, and Lanquer, Robert: Tourisme et environnement en Méditerranée. Enjeux et prospec-
      tive, Economica, Paris, 1995

78   Ashdown Environmental Limited: Water supply and sewage disposal specialist study,
      November 1993

79   Boers, H. and M. Bosch: The earth as a holiday resort. An introduction to tourism and the
      environment, Utrecht, 1994, p 60

involved in disposing of solid waste.

Most of the waste has been placed in land deposits or shipped to the mainland. Over the last few years "green point stations" have been established to allow tourists and in- habitants to separate their waste into - typically - two or three fragments. The separated waste (for instance glass) has been shipped to the mainland for recycling. Only a small proportion of the total amount of solid waste is recycled. In 1996, an incineration plant was put into operation in order to change the critical practice of solid waste treatment.

However, this plant was heavily opposed by environmental organizations, for instance Friends of the Earth and GOB (Grupo Balear d'Ornitologia i Defensa de la Naturalesa). They are doubtful that the plant will meet high enough emission standards in regard to, e.g. dioxins. If such standards are not met the environmental organizations fear that land deposits will be preferred. Furthermore, GOB especially is working towards the introduction of much more radical recycling programmes, as - without exception - recycling is considered the most environmentally friendly solution.

As planned, the incineration plant produces electricity as a by-product, since no district heating system exists which might efficiently exploit a by-product such as heat.

Separation and avoidance of waste are measures widely accepted by tourists on Mallorca. Around 90 per cent in summer as well as in winter and of all nationalities consider initiatives of this kind sensible, and they are willing to contribute towards alleviating the environmental waste problems.

3.3.6. Energy supply

GESA is the monopoly public service producing and distributing electricity to the consumers and industries of Mallorca. The production input consists of oil and carbon.

In spite of higher prices, consumption has increased over the last few years. Tourists' demand for more comfort - for instance air conditioning - is one of the reasons for the increase in demand.

As a result of a programme of incentives aimed at the introduction of solar energy, a small number of hotels and private homes have installed solar energy equipment to provide hot water. The programme has been subsequently closed down. Given the solar energy potential available on Mallorca, the exploitation of this source of energy is at a very low level. Renewable energy (all types) accounts for 5.4 per cent of total energy consumption on the Balearic Islands which is less than one fifth of what is potentially possible[80].

Energy supply and efficiency is not as much of an issue in the environmental debate on Mallorca as waste treatment and water supply. For instance, the subject was not included in the ECOMOST survey. Some measures to save energy were, however, recommended.

Earlier in this chapter it was shown that the predominant means of transportation to Mallorca is air transport - the most energy consuming mode of transportation. On the other hand, the concentrated tourist urbanization limits the need for internal transportation on the island. This structure is also appropriate for an efficient public transport system in the Palma area. The tour operators undertake a large proportion of the transportation needed in connection with transits and sightseeing in buses, although the trend towards individualization has caused a boom in the car rental sector. Bicycles play only a very small role as a means of transport.

3.3.7. Conclusions

Environmental constraints arising in consequence of tourism are predominantly concentrated in the following areas:

- Water-shortages, and the effects caused by an over-exploitation of scarce resources (salination, lowering of the ground water table, etc.).

- The built-up environment. With its high densities this is degrading and needs restructuring and refurbishment. From an environmental point of view this concentration is, however, not an entirely negative feature.

- Emissions related to transportation. These emissions are caused by the fact that Mallorca is an island destination attracting tourists travelling by aeroplane.

- Waste water and solid waste handling problems. These are being tackled by the authorities, but must be considered far from solved.

The water situation in particular will become utterly critical if the pressure exerted by

---

80   IDAE (Instituto para la Diversificacion y Ahorro de la Energia): Guía de las Energías Renovables en Baleares/4, 1995

tourism is increased. The authorities and environmental organizations consider even the present level environmentally unsustainable in certain coastal areas.

Other sectors of industry or activities cannot be said to have a negative influence on tourism on Mallorca. But its location in the Mediterranean eco-system renders Mallorca very dependent on other nations' attitudes towards the marine environment.

3.4. The environmental regulation system

3.4.1. Authorities

The 1978 constitution recognized and guaranteed the "historic nationalities" and regions which formed the unified nation of Spain the right to autonomy. Seventeen self-governing Autonomous Regions were formed of which the Balearic Islands is one. Each region has its own statutes. Regions have Legislative Assemblies and Governing Councils with executive and administrative powers.

A great deal of Spanish environmental legislation was developed in the 1980s and is therefore not particularly firmly established in the Spanish legal system[81]. The Spanish constitution does, however, state that the Autonomous Regions should assume responsibility for the management of the environment, and that the government is exclusively responsible for basic environmental legislation. Basic legislation is only concerned with the mountains, the exploitation of forests and cattle trails, the comprehensive management of water resources and the sea and coastline.

There is no direct protection of the environment in the civil code - it deals with the liabilities for damages arising out of certain of conduct. Pombo also states that the regulations contained in the penal code are somewhat inadequate in regard to the wider aspects of environmental protection[82]. New legislation will, however, regulate planning offences more rigorously than before, including unauthorized construction of buildings.

According to the basic ideas behind the independence of the Spanish regions, the regional government is the most important authority when it comes to regulating,

---

81   Pombo, Fernando: Spain in Brealey, Mark (ed): Environmental Liabilities and Regulation in Europe, International Business Publishing Limited, The Hague, 1992, pp 405-431

82   Ibid.

planning and controlling the environment. The regional government issues its own laws, some of which will affect the tourism sector, and the regional authorities are also in charge of making legislative efforts aimed at changing the structure of the industry.

The municipalities are in charge of local land-use planning. These plans are, however, subject to approval by the regional government. The municipalities must regulate in detail expansion of the tourist areas and check whether building activities comply with plans and restrictions. The municipalities own and take care of the beach infrastructure, roads, promenades, etc., and normally the local authorities are also in charge of the treatment of solid waste and waste water.

Over the last few years there has been a tendency for the Balearic Regional Government to manifest its regulatory powers more actively, not only in order to protect the environment of the island, but also to ensure the creation of a new platform for the development of tourism towards a new competitiveness and away from self-destruction.

This development does not only comply with the principles of decentralization adopted by the Spanish National Government, but also reflects the realization that for many years environmental protection has been insufficient[83].

3.4.2. Regulation by laws, plans and standards

As tourism has many facets, regulatory initiatives can be found within a number of different regulatory frameworks. This is also the case on Mallorca. The following are of particular importance to tourism.

- The *Law on Planning of the Territory*[84] aims at a co-ordinated planning of the area. This co-ordination formalizes a planning hierarchy where more detailed plans are provided by the municipalities. This was the first planning law ever, and since it was passed, a considerable amount of work has been done by the Govern Balear to fill in the framework with practical action plans and follow-up legislation. "Sustainability" is included in the

---

83   Tarrio, Filipe Ruza: Organizational structure, Spain in European Environmental Yearbook, 1990, pp 341-342; and Avelino Blasco: Legislacion Turistica de Baleares, supplement to the ECOMOST project

84   Ley 8/1987, de 1 de abril, de Ordenación Territorial de las Islas Baleares

title of the planning documents.

Four "planning instruments" have been institutionalized:

*   The guidelines of land-use planning (Las Directrices de Ordenación Territorial - DOT)

*   Partial land-use plans (Los Planes Territoriles Parciales)

*   Sectoral plans (los Planes Directores Sectoriales), and

*   Land-use planning for natural areas (los Planes de Ordenación del Medio Natural)[85].

The "DOT" guidelines include an ambitious development strategy and comprehensive planning. Parts of DOT and some of the legislative follow-up initiatives are of particular importance in connection with the issue of sustainable tourism. For instance the *regulation of building activities in protected areas*[86]. The protected areas can be divided into three categories:

*   Areas given the highest protection priority, which consist of coasts, dunes, some mountain areas, very small islands, some forest areas, etc. In these areas it is prohibited to erect new buildings, unless they are part of approved town plans. New golf courses and marinas are not allowed.

*   Areas of particular natural interest, which form the major part of the areas that have been placed under protection. The mode of regulation applied here is very different from the one mentioned above. In these areas new buildings are allowed; each unit should, however, be attached to a plot of land of at least 20 hectares. In addition, the buildings should be adapted to local building techniques and materials and should be no more than two storeys high. Golf courses and marinas are not allowed.

*   Areas with valuable scenic qualities that are primarily traditional

---

85   Govern Balear: DOT Islas Baleares. Hacia un Desarrollo Sostenible del Territorio, n.d.

86   Ley de los espacios naturales, metioned in Govern Balear: Gesetz über Naturlandschaften gemäss städtebaulichen Regelungen für besonders geschützte Zonen der Balearen, pamphlet

agricultural landscapes. The same measures as above apply, but the minimum plot size is only three hectares.

The strategy applied to regulate natural areas comes close to a *dispersion strategy* - less harm done if there are fewer buildings. This mode of regulation is very much in tune with the proprietors' strong sense of ownership, as mentioned above.

- The *EIA (Environmental Impact Assessment)* obligation will be implemented by means of a decree in 1998. But as early as in 1986 the Balearic Government described the types of projects that would be subject to EIA and placed them on two lists: the first list includes those projects that require a detailed evaluation, and the second list contains the projects that will only have to be subjected to a simplified evaluation[87].

A number of EIAs have been performed. In practice, EIAs are carried out by the developers, not the authorities. The local environmental groups do not consider EIAs worthy of their undivided respect.

- The *Tourism Supply Regulation Plan* (Pla de Ordenació de l'Oferta Turìstica, POOT) which was approved in the shape of a decree on April 6, 1995 is presently regarded as the most important initiative when it comes to regulating tourism and thus achieving sustainability. This plan was considered very controversial - which can be seen from the fact that it took sic years to gain approval[88].

The POOT embraces a number of broad goals such as the prevention of coastal sprawl, co-ordination of tourism and town planning, limitation of tourism development, setting standards of quality and supporting alternative forms of tourism.

Among the most important measures was the strengthening of the requirements applying to new hotels. Before the approval of the POOT, the land-use standard applied was 30 square metres of land per tourist bed, POOT, however, stipulates a standard of 60 square metres per bed, thus

---

87   Alvarez, Antonio Garcia: Environmental impact assessment, Spain in European Environmental Yearbook, 1990

88   Robledo, Marco Antonio and Julio Batle: Integral tourism re-planning in a mature destination: Mallorca's POOT, unpublished paper, n.d.

facilitating a future lower density in the tourist districts.

Furthermore, POOT institutionalizes the requirement that hotels should have 4 or 5 stars - in order to discourage the cheapest modes of holiday-making. In addition, developers are encouraged to ensure the establishment fixes minimum areas dedicated for sports facilities, parking, green areas and swimming pools. The hotels should stand on a minimum plot of land of 12,000 square metres, and they should have at least 300 beds.

POOT defined 37 tourist areas, for each of which specific ratios of development are suggested. The ratios reflect sustainability criteria such as the availability of fresh water supplies, beach areas, infrastructure, etc.

As part of this legislative reform, the local authorities are required to adapt their spatial planning to the POOT. The real impact of the POOT in terms of lower densities and better quality will probably not make itself felt within this decade, as numerous approved but still unused planning permissions do not comply with the new standards. The authorities will, however, attempt to re-negotiate these permissions, although they are aware that developers will forward compensation claims. Financial limitations will reduce the authorities' possibilities for ensuring that the POOT objectives can be obtained by negotiation.

- The *Coastal Law (Ley de Costas)* of 1988 is a national law aimed at the protection of the marine and land heritage. At the regional level it is co-ordinated with initiatives to protect the natural environment and the regulation of the construction activities in these areas.

The Coastal Law establishes an obligation to protect the sea (the 100 metres zone), i.e. transit and access regulations. (In regard to automobile traffic access, points must be 500 metres apart, and for pedestrians the distance is 200 metres). A "zone of influence" of at least 500 metres has also been defined: from the coastline and inland - a rule which could modify the nature of land and urban planning. Discharging solid waste and raw sewage is prohibited in the protected areas[89].

The Coastal Law has been included in the Balearic regulations, along with the above-mentioned initiatives.

---

89   Tarrio, Filipe Ruza: Sea/Coast, Spain in European Environmental Handbook, 1990

- The *Hotel Modernization Law (Ley de 30.5.1990 de Modernizacion de Alojamientos Touristicos)* is a Balearic law which is designed to ensure continual upgrading of the technical and safety standards of the hotels. Only hotels opened before June 1984 are included in the strict inspection procedures performed by independent inspectors. However, this law is not specifically concerned with environmental matters, although some of the issues touch upon what is considered important in relation to sustainability on Mallorca.

   The law is quite clear when it comes to penalties. If the technical requirements are not met by hoteliers, their licences will be withdrawn.

In regard to energy supply and consumption, there is only limited national legislation, primarily of a technical nature and aimed at the regulation of concessions. No comprehensive planning is required. In February 1995, the Balearic Government launched a decree on the diversification of energy consumption and ways to increase renewable energy resources[90].

Environmental regulation and planning are recent phenomena, some of which were adopted as a result of joining the EU. The regional governments do not want the popular opinion in the EU that they are lagging behind in these respects to become too firmly established. The Balearic Islands in particular are attempting to promote themselves as "pilot" and "advanced" areas, pioneers of quality and sustainable tourism.

The constitutional set-up makes regional autonomous initiatives possible. Bearing in mind the small size of the municipalities, however, it is primarily the regional governments that possess the powers and the competencies to work for sustainable tourism by means of introducing the appropriate regulations.

In spite of plans, formal powers and competency Mallorca envisages problems of execution, as commented upon by the IFTO[91]. Previous permissions are blocking the direct route to new ideas and concepts. In addition, illegal activities are not easily combatted in a society with only recent traditions of regulation.

---

90   IDAE (Instituto para la Diversificacion y Ahorro de la Energia): Guía de las Energías Renovables en Baleares/4, 1995

91   IFTO: Planning for sustainable tourism. The ECOMOST project, Lewes, n.d.

3.4.3. Regulation by means of financial instruments

Green taxes are unknown phenomena in Spain and Mallorca. Employing the price mechanism with the immediate aim of reducing the consumption of scarce resources and of creating revenues is something that does not take place.

In an indirect way, scarcity has an effect on prices. Thus the tourism industry is encouraged to save energy, water etc., as the costs are high. The supply system is handled by public monopolies, but they are obliged to fix their prices in such a way that their costs are covered, but they are not supposed to generate revenues. Differentiated pricing structures - such as for instance extra charges to be paid by tourist facilities as opposed to private households - have not been applied everywhere on the island. In the municipality of Calvia large consumers are, however, punished via a progressive scale of prices for water and waste treatment. There are also agreements with the hoteliers to collect separated waste, which will give hotels financial benefits.

There are no tourist levies (kurtax) on Mallorca to cover expenses incurred in connection with environmental protection and the provision of infrastructure. Where construction of new hotels is concerned, the municipalities can charge a licence fee of 4% of the estimated building costs. These licences have been and still are a source of revenue of some importance. As long as these licences are a means of finance, municipalities cannot be expected unambiguously to support strategies to slow down the tourist inflows and lower the densities of the tourist areas.

Using regulatory forces, the POOT does, however, attempt to compensate for the counteracting financial incentives. Nevertheless, if speedy implementation of the POOT is to be ensured, supplementary financing will be needed. A total sum of 60,000m pesetas (about US$ 500m) will be required to remove 40,000 hotel rooms from the market and to implement other measures. Financial means are necessary to buy and tear down property and to compensate developers for applying lower densities, etc. Financing POOT is problematic, and no solution has been found so far. One option which has been debated is to create a kurtax system to co-finance the POOT. A differentiation of payments according to the environmental constraints caused has also been suggested. According to this model, high-rise hotels close to the coastline, with small green areas, etc., would have to pay heavier charges than less environmentally hostile establishments[92]. Public finances from the regional

---

92   Robledo, Marco Antonio and Julio Batle: Integral tourism re-planning in a mature destination: Mallorca's POOT, unpublished paper, n.d.

government will be made available to cover 33 per cent of the costs of POOT - but only if private financing can be found to fill the gap and cover the total costs.

Mallorca used to be an EU Objective 1 region, a region which is "lagging behind", where support was provided to adjust its development, and at the same time a region where rural areas would need restructuring. The inflow of EU subsidies has helped to launch numerous projects, in particular in regard to the provision of infrastructure.

Without the EU, plus national and regional subsidies, the municipality of Calvia would probably not have initiated its ambitious sea front renovation project involving the beaches, beach infrastructure, promenades, parks, etc. The effect on the tourism industry is indirect, but considered important as a demonstration of how to achieve favourable development. The image of the resort is expected to improve in the minds of the tourists, and this initiative will, in addition, set an example to business proprietors proving that improvements and environmental renovation bring benefits[93].

Investment subsidies for private proprietors have not been particularly successful on Mallorca. For instance, the regional government ran a programme to promote the installation of solar energy. The lack of demand from proprietors resulted in the programme having to be closed down. Technical problems caused by high salt content in fresh water constitute a parallel reason explaining the lack of success of this particular programme.

At present, subsidies are allocated for the conversion of a limited number of farm houses which can then be used tourism purposes. This initiative is usually mentioned as complying with the ideas of sustainability in spite of the fact that it might contribute to an expansion of the accommodation capacity of the island. The justification underlying these subsidies is that they may help to preserve agricultural landscapes and building styles.

To conclude - this section shows that the use of green taxes and financial incentives to deflect the direction of the development process towards sustainability is fairly infrequent on Mallorca. However, the severe problems encountered in financing the ambitious goals of POOT have indeed provoked debate about which financial measures can be used to supplement other types of measures.

The authorities are very much aware that the unloading of still more costs onto

---

93   Ajuntament de Calvià: First operation of Calvià's desaturation plan, n.d.

accommodation owners will have a negative effect on competitiveness. This is stated as the main reason for the reluctance to implement further taxation.

3.4.4. Collaborative and behavioural measures

In this section a number of voluntary and collaborative environmental initiatives will be outlined. These initiatives are organized by the tourism industry, the tourist associations, the authorities and/or other organizations.

First, two "eco-label" initiatives will be mentioned. The Municipality of Alcudia was the first initiator to launch an eco-tourism campaign, the core of which was the eco-labelling of local hotel establishments and public investments in renovation and infrastructure. At a tourist fair as early as in 1992, the community declared itself an eco-tourism destination, and the Municipality committed itself to work for this goal by initiating a number of co-ordinated activities[94].

The first step was an "internal marketing drive" designed to promote the idea among the population and the hoteliers and their staff. Furthermore, the tourist association of Alcudia presented the project to selected tour operators and secured recommendations to be used as additional internal propaganda material to help fix the criteria of the eco-label. A committee under the city council is in charge of awarding eco-labels.

By Autumn 1995, two hotels had received an eco-label, indicating that they satisfy 13 sustainability criteria. The pioneering hotels found that co-operation with the city council on this matter looked promising; the attempt to communicate the idea to the tour operators was especially welcomed. However, some other hoteliers are more reserved. They fear that they will not be able to fulfil the criteria. One section in particular stipulating that at least 40% of the plot should be dedicated to green areas will cause difficulties to a large number of the 70 hotels in Alcudia.

To sum-up the eco-label project in Alcudia: although it was initiated by the city council in order to create a green destination, it has, nevertheless, been difficult to unify the interests of the local tourism industry and bring them to give their full support to the project.

---

94 Ajuntament d'Alcúdia: Satzung des Ausschusses für die Förderung und Bewilligung der Ökotouristischen Plaketten, n.d.; and TUI: Urlaub und Umwelt Mallorca, n.d.

Recently, the regional government decided to launch a more comprehensive eco-labelling programme, "Programa Ecotur"[95]. This programme has four sub-programmes:

- "Ecoauditur": setting up of an eco-audit organization with the relevant technical capacities. This organization is to operate according to EU approved regulations and to ensure the consistent auditing and awarding of eco-labels to the tourism industry.

- "Coetur": establishing eco-awareness among all relevant persons within the field of tourism, i.e. the industry, the local authorities, the tour operators, the tourists. This part of the programme is for instance to result in the preparation of codes of conduct, image campaigns, etc.

- "Secotur": development of green destinations, i.e. a more comprehensive and complex eco-auditing activity.

- "Apecotur": designing auxiliary tools to be used in the above programmes, for instance, GIS (geographical information systems), subject information systems, multimedia remedies, etc.

In this case, the authorities have been the initiators, while the local tourism industry and its organizations have been less active. This does not mean that the tourism industry does not want any influence on the matter, but that it prefers to operate along other channels or to be independent.

According to the authorities, the industry cannot be characterized as being particularly "proactive" when it comes to environmental measures. Fierce conditions of competition and the general excess capacity discourages hoteliers from undertaking risky investments. Even minor investments which have proved financially feasible and investments with a very short pay-back period - such as water saving aggregates - have not been globally installed. A survey by IFTO showed that the measures introduced in hotels amounted to the following[96]:

---

95   The programme bases itself on the EU initiative to promote voluntary eco-auditing: European Union, Regulation no. 1836/93 allowing voluntary participation by companies in the industrial sector in a Community eco-management and audit scheme, OJ.C 168/1, CEC, Luxembourg, 1993

96   IFTO: Planning for sustainable development, The Ecomost Project, n.d.

Environmentally-friendly laundry and dry cleaning:	63% of hotels
Saving energy and water:	49% of hotels
Avoiding waste, waste disposal and recycling:	48% of hotels
Environmentally-friendly construction:	42% of hotels
Information supplied to staff and guests:	39% of hotels
Environmentally-friendly transport policy:	31% of hotels

The report mentions some reservations concerning the hotels' reliability in this matter. Seriousness and comprehensiveness of planning and management is lacking in a great number of enterprises.

The upper section of the hotels, which is dominated primarily by chains, is more aware of the opportunities that may be gained by engaging in some "proactive" behaviour. However, they run their own eco-initiatives, as they are not dependent on community provided systems such as the Alcudia eco-hotels.

The hoteliers' associations have strongly recommended the POOT programme, mostly because it would result in no more capacity being added to the hotel market. However, willingness to undertake investment to fulfil the remaining intentions of POOT is more limited.

Together with the construction sector, the hoteliers' associations form a very influential force in Mallorcan society, and their opinions carry great weight in the political system. Their non-involvement in the sustainability projects can also be seen as an indicator of the fact that environmental matters are not yet considered crucial to business. Mallorcan tourism is still "old-fashioned"[97] - "Here today, gone tomorrow" rather than "See and enjoy, but do not destroy". The "old" tourist attitudes still influence the hoteliers.

However, the hoteliers and their associations are eager to supplement their product with, for instance golf courses and marinas, because they see these facilities as assets of diversification and opportunities for expanding the tourist season. In an environmental sense these do, nevertheless, constitute a dilemma. While less pronounced seasonal fluctuations will in some respects alleviate environmental constraints, the golf facilities - for instance - do also give rise to severe problems,

---

97   Poon, Auliana: Tourism, technology and competitive strategies, CAB International, Walling-
        ford, 1993, p.10

such as water and pesticide problems. The nature of the political decision-making process preceding their establishment is not always beyond critical comment. Boers and Bosch note the following: "For instance, the law on nature conservation has been changed after only a year: following a political change of course the government decided to revoke the protected status of a number of areas. Since then, these areas have seen particularly intensive development. For instance, dozens of chalets have been built in a former saltpan, a nature reserve that had all the features of a valuable wetland".[98]

The economic importance of tourism and the construction industry is the major factor explaining why it is possible to influence the political processes and why it can be brought to bear so forcefully. The efforts of the regional government to diversify the economy can be seen as an attempt to moderate the influence of the tourism industry and to redirect the interests of the construction sector. Public investments in university buildings, resort infrastructure, airport facilities, etc. are expected to have the same effect.

To conclude: the tourism industry has a number of reasons for hesitating when it comes to participating in the sustainability project. It could even be said to have an interest in obstructing these policies. This is the reason why alliances with (foreign) tour operators have become so important to the regional and local authorities.

Tour operators are the intermediaries between the customers and the owners of the tourism products at the destinations. The bargaining power of the tour operators vis-à-vis the hoteliers is staggering. Yet, at the same time, the tour operators take an interest in keeping up the standard and image of destinations which have been marketed successfully for many years. The destinations represent marketing investments which have certain pay-back periods.

No wonder, then, that the German tour operators - especially TUI and Neckermann - have taken the lead in the sustainability debate, and that the local authorities and environmental organizations on Mallorca co-operate with them and other tour operators. TUI subjects some destinations to an environmental audit, and the company engages hoteliers and authorities in discussions to discover what elements they find

---

98   Boers, H. og M. Bosch: The earth as a holiday resort. An introduction to tourism and the environment, Utrecht, 1994, p 66

particularly critical[99]. IFTO, the International Federation of Tour Operators, launched the ECOMOST project in which Mallorca serves as a case study region. The ECOMOST project is well-known throughout Mallorca, and the interest shown by IFTO has indeed challenged the Balearic Government to launch the more comprehensive ECOTUR programme.

The GOB (Grup d'Ornitologia Balear) and Friends of the Earth are the most active environmental grassroots organizations on Mallorca. Friends of the Earth have adopted a co-operative strategy, for instance by preparing guideline pamphlets to be distributed via hotel lobbies. This initiative was undertaken in co-operation with the British tour operator, Thompson. Friends of the Earth have also developed a video on environmentally friendly tourist behaviour which is shown by British Airways as part of their inflight film programme. Finally, this organization initiated co-operative relations with the local university to establish a formal sustainable tourism course at managerial level.

The GOB is more radical and critical in its choice of main issues, and this organization focuses particularly on cases involving the destruction of natural resources and cultural heritage. More pragmatically, GOB was also involved in the staff training programmes of the Alcudia eco-label project[100].

None of these organizations feels that the influence of NGOs is sufficient to provoke the necessary change of policies; the GOB finds that it is being marginalized in the political process[101].

When it comes to supplying tourists with information about the environment no comprehensive strategies can be found. The Balearic Government publishes pamphlets with information about such natural resources as vulnerable species. The existence of particular areas of interest is most often described in tourist brochures published by the municipalities or the region. As walking and biking have become more popular, guides have been prepared by the authorities in order to inform people of available opportunities. Most often these brochures and pamphlets do not contain detailed "eco-

---

99   Iwand, Michael (TUI): Instruments, procedures and experiences of integrating the environment into tourism development by a major tour operator, paper at the World Conference on Sustainable Tourism, Lanzarote, April 1995

100   Coll Perello, Margarita: Turismo y medio ambiente: Hacia un turismo compatible, student dissertation, Universitat de las Islas Baleares, n.d.

101   IFTO: Planning for sustainable tourism. The ECOMOST Project, n.d.

ethics", codes of conduct, or guidelines to be followed by the visitors.

There are no visitor centres or museums dedicated to the communication of environmental issues on Mallorca, except the natural park centre of S'Albufera.

3.4.5. Conclusions on environmental regulatory instruments

The above sections contained an analysis of 1) regulation by means of laws and plans, 2) regulation via financial instruments, and 3) regulation by means of collaborative efforts and information. Taking an overall view encompassing all of these instruments, the following can be concluded:

- Environmental regulation has only very recently been incorporated into Mallorcan policy. No groups of instruments nor any of the single instruments can be claimed to be particularly well-developed at the moment. The co-ordination of instruments is weak. Comprehensive policies are in their preparatory phase. However, these past few years, the adoption of a number of instruments has been accelerated.

- Within the field of environmental regulation the emphasis has been placed on the development of laws and plans, as a response to the previous void of strategically motivated instruments of this type. The use of financial instruments in environmental regulation has not been prepared and adopted, neither in Mallorca, nor in a national framework.

- The fact of the interrelationship between business interests and politics is well-known on Mallorca. This tradition is, however, hampering rather than promoting the idea of an environmentally sustainable future for the island. The hoteliers hesitate, primarily in regard to supporting initiatives which they are not supposed to co-finance or in which they see only a short-term financial interest. There are powerful business lobbies, but there is no equally powerful environmental lobby. This lack of response from the locals creates a vacuum - a vacuum which is occupied by foreign tour operators (particularly Geman ones).

The emphasis is on formal regulation, but it is very important to note that the contents of these regional and municipal regulations and plans are subject to considerable business influence. In some instances, co-operation with the influential business sector has led to their being in favour of sustainable development, but more often the opposite is the case.

Therefore, those advocating sustainable development are not primarily found *on* the island, but rather *outside* it. That the tour operators have now become the agents of change illustrates the fact that the market now requires the Mallorcans to operate at a faster pace.

In certain ways, the constitution represents an obstacle to action. A representative of the National Directorate of the Coast mentions that the great problems encountered in coastal management are the result of the distribution of executive power among the autonomous governments[102]. Also EU regulations aimed at recovering environmental values have in some cases got stuck in the administrative system, for instance the Environmental Impact Assessment obligation.

Finally, it must be mentioned that the population on Mallorca - including the staff of the tourism enterprises - is sceptical about at least one of the major issues of the sustainability project: the upper limit on the tourist inflow. Jobs and incomes depend so much on tourism, and the population's attitude towards tourism is predominantly favourable[103]. Anybody wanting to scale down the volume of tourism is bound to run into problems.

A marketing plan recently presented argues that the ceiling restricting the number of tourism arrivals should be fixed at 11 million (compared to the 1995 level of 8.4 million) *on the condition* that the handling of environmental problems is improved and that the seasonality problems are addressed.

3.5. Environmental innovations

Below a number of innovative efforts initiated as a consequence of environmental regulations will be discussed.

3.5.1. The elimination of the Hotel Playa Palma Nova

An important element of the desaturation plan of the municipality of Calvia was the elimination of the Hotel Playa Palma Nova. The hotel was the first hotel to be

---

102   Friends of the Earth, Mednet: Sustainable tourism in the Mediterranean, n.d.

103   The 4 Towns Project - 1993. Analisis Cuestionario Residentes Alcudia

established in Palma Nova, and it opened its doors to the public in 1960.

This hotel had been built directly on the beach, and it represented an obstacle to the ambitious seafront renovation project. The removal of this obstacle opened up certain possibilities, e.g. the creation of a continuous promenade and green areas. Its surface area was close to 4,000 square metres, and its demolition caused 46 hotel rooms to be taken out of business.

Seen in comparison to the surplus of several hundred thousand hotel rooms, and many square kilometres of outmoded tourist resorts, the importance of the Hotel Playa Palma Nova is negligible. The decision to blow it up did, however, have a symbolic value, which significantly exceeded its small size.

On 1 April 1995, the demolition took place in the presence of the Minister of Tourism and Commerce, Sr. Javier Gómez Navarro, and of the world's press.

This "big bang" echoed in the press of all the home countries of the tourists to Mallorca. The effects this "dramatic" measure would have on the island's image was considered much more valuable than small - even costly - steps towards sustainability.

3.5.2. Eco-labelling of the Hotel Bahia de Alcudia

The Hotel Bahia de Alcudia was the first hotel to be awarded the Alcudia "Hoteles Ecoturisticos" label. This took place in 1995 after a long period of preparation.

The conditions laid down in the eco-labelling rules point out the crucial importance of saving fresh water. A reduction of at least 25% is required. In order to reach this target, the hotelier installed water saving equipment in all bathrooms. Furthermore, recycled laundry water is used for the irrigation of the hotel gardens. As a result, up to 50% less water is now used than was previously the case.

The hotelier was a pioneer in regard to investigating the qualities of different types of water saving equipment. Some salt - of which substantial amounts can be found in fresh water on Mallorca - collects in the tap, and the passage of the water is easily blocked. Equipment able to cope with these difficult conditions and technical requirements was eventually found.

After a period of intensive experiments, co-operative relations were established between the hotelier and the the manufacturer of his choice in order to exploit the experience gained for a mutual marketing effort. The manufacturer uses the hotel as a "demonstration" object, and the hotel enjoys the advantage of being able to promote itself and its activities.

3.5.3. ECOTUR

As mentioned earlier in this chapter, the ECOTUR programme aims at a systematic eco-auditing and eco-labelling of Mallorcan tourist facilities and resorts. In particular the auxiliary programme of Apecotur may turn out to have wider perspectives.

The plans for Apecotur include the development of information material based on multimedia. By the end of 1995, environmental management software will be launched and offered to hotels.

Furthermore, the application of a GIS system will ensure the co-ordination of area planning, environmental management and information.

Telematic interconnections between persons/institutions within the field of environmental management will be created in order to share information more efficiently.

The last strand will be the upgrading of tourist guides and information material concerning the environment - a particularly important task. One of the issues will be to find a means of communication with Mallorca's mass market. A tourist volume of six million per year (many of whom have no particular understanding of or interest in the environmental problems) will require a different strategy of communication than mere pamphlets.

ECOTUR is a pioneering project in the sense that it represents the first tourism application of the European framework on eco-audits. During 1996 a diagnosis will be made at 25 hotels, using the manuals and other material developed by ECOTUR. Subsequently, the municipalities will undergo a similar procedure. The budget of ECOTUR is 400 million pesetas, partly financed by the EU Life programme.

4. Isle of Wight

4.1. Introduction

The British island, Isle of Wight, has been included as a case study region in this project concerned with environmental regulation in the tourism sector. The assumption is that regulations as embedded in law and tradition will cause constraints to arise in the enterprise sector but that they will also provide the sector with opportunities. It is further anticipated that British regulatory legislation and traditions differ from those in the other regions studied. Accordingly, sustainable tourism may turn out to be a different type of issue on the Isle of Wight than on Bornholm in Denmark and Mallorca in Spain.

The term regulation should be broadly interpreted, so as to embrace legal initiatives and planning as well as voluntary actions launched by the tourism industry or other agents within the field of tourism.

When researching for this case study it was considered crucial to identify particularly innovative business responses to the regulatory forces. Innovations within the field of sustainable tourism do not only consist of setting "best practice" examples to other enterprises, they must be seen as especially significant cases that exist before an understanding of the dynamics leading towards higher levels of sustainability can emerge. Conversely, the lack of obvious innovations is also a key to analysis of the nature of regulation.

Section 4.2. of this chapter gives a brief description of the tourist situation on the Isle of Wight. In section 4.3. particular emphasis is placed on the most important environmental problems on the island. The regulatory system is described in section 4.4., and the last part of this section deals with the innovative aspects of sustainable tourism. Conclusions and perspectives will be deferred until chapter 5, which includes a comparative analysis of the greening of tourism in the three case study islands.

4.2. The importance of tourism to the island

The Isle of Wight is located in the English Channel south of Great Britain. The distance separating the island from the mainland is short - ferry transport by catamaran takes only 15 minutes from Portsmouth to Ryde. Travelling time on vehicle ferries is still only 30-60 minutes depending on the port of departure.

The Isle of Wight has a surface area of about 330 square kilometres, and the population is about 124,800[104]. From 1981 to 1993 the population rose by 5.7 per cent. A considerable part of this growth was related to a retirement trend: for a long period the Isle of Wight has been a popular place to go after retiring from the labour market. The climate is one of the best to be found in England, and the place is attractive to persons who have reasons not to want to leave the UK. The proportion of inhabitants above the retirement age amounts to 26.5 per cent on the Isle of Wight compared to the British average of 18.2 per cent[105].

There are no overall statistics on tourist bednights or arrivals. However, studies undertaken by the English Tourist Board in 1981 and by PA Consultants in 1994 give estimates that are accurate enough to allow conclusions to be drawn about the most dominant characteristics and about the development of tourism on the island[106].

Table 4.1. Changes in volume between 1981 and 1993 (June to September only)

	1981	1993	Change
Long holiday trips	664,000	385,000	-42%
Short break trips	136,000	153,000	+13%
All tourism trips	800,000	538,000	-33%
Day visits	600,000	484,000	-20%
Holiday nights	6,600,000	3,529,000	-46%

Adapted from PA Consultants, 1994

---

104   Central Statistical Office: Regional trends, 1995 edition, London, 1995

105   Ibid.

106   PA Consultants: Isle of Wight visitor survey, May 1994 and English Tourist Board: Isle of Wight Tourism Study, September 1981

94

The table, which is based on the two surveys mentioned above, indicates a substantial fall in the volume of tourist activities over the period between 1981 and 1993. When distinguishing between two segments of arrivals, long holidays and short breaks, it can be seen that in 1993 long holidays were still dominant. But since 1981, a considerable decline has taken place within this segment. The short break market has on the other hand increased, but far from enough to compensate. 1993 and 1994 surveys show that tourism levels have stabilized[107], but the day-trip market declined during the 1980s and the early 1990s.

The declining volume in the long holiday market on the Isle of Wight has resulted in an even more crucial decrease in the total number of holiday bednights. The impact of this structural change in the holiday market is very significant.

The 1981 survey concludes that "the great popularity of the Isle of Wight as a holiday destination is confirmed... The volume of tourism on the island is ... equivalent to that of the largest English tourist resorts"[108]. Subsequent surveys do, however, indicate that the island has not been able to keep pace with holiday-makers' changing expectations. The island has failed to grasp potential lucrative markets[109].

In seeking to understand the reasons for the development of tourism on the island, the market surveys and strategy documents available are valuable sources. First, the majority of tourists on the Isle of Wight are British (around 93 per cent). The island has the image of a typical English tourist resort, and the number of foreigners does not seem to have increased. Cheap packaged coach tours have grown in importance. This has helped to increase bed occupancy, but to the tourism industry on the island it is only a question of small margins. The ferry companies are also operating packaged tour departments. The revenues from this type of business are lower thus leading to a combined "blessing and blight" effect in the accommodation sector on the island.

Secondly, when Queen Victoria established her summer residence on the island, the Isle

---

107   Southern Tourist Board, Visitor Research Service: Isle of Wight Strategy Research 1994, May 1994. This survey includes all seasons, but the same trends can be identified as in the two other studies referred to.

108   English Tourist Board: Isle of Wight Tourism Study, September 1981, p i

109   Isle of Wight Tourism and Southern Tourist Board: Isle of Wight tourism strategy, April 1994

of Wight became a fashionable resort. The Queen was followed by the celebrities of her time. Since the glory days of the Victorian period, the many large houses and residences have been converted into hotels and guest houses. Around 2,000 establishments provide accommodation for tourists, 60 per cent of which boast less than 10 bedrooms. Only 13 hotels have more than 50 bedrooms. Most of these houses are not entirely fitted for their purpose, and they have had severe difficulties maintaining modern standards. A significant number of the guest houses are owned by people who entered into business late in life, i.e. in connection with their retirement from a paid job. Often they do not have any professional qualifications and training, and their level of ambition in terms of change and growth is often low.

Self-catering establishments are also predominantly small-scale operations with 80 per cent of them having less than five units[110].

This particular structure of the industry in combination with the extraordinary retirement pattern has had a negative influence on the tourists' image of the island causing a continuous downward trend. In recent decades the island has appealed especially to low/middle income families.

Third, understanding of the situation of Isle of Wight tourism is bound up with its facilities as well as with its image. The island has the reputation of being geared towards families with children and senior citizens, and young people find that there is not enough to "see and do". The Isle of Wight is a "bucket and spade destination". Evidence from the surveys confirms that the younger generations tend to prefer other holiday destinations.

Fourthly, the character of the tourism and the difficulties encountered are both close related to the issue of seasonality. Two-thirds of accommodation facilities are not open in the off-season. Figure 4.1. shows the number of 1993 arrivals on a per month basis, demonstrating the seasonality of the tourism on the island.

---

110   Isle of Wight Tourism and Southern Tourist Board: Isle of Wight Tourism Strategy, April
        1994

Figure 4.1. Visitor crossings per month to the Isle of Wight, 1993

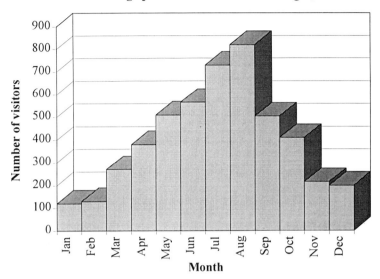

Source: PA Consultants: Isle of Wight visitor survey, May 1994

July and August are the peak months with around six times as many visitors as in January and February. Even in the peak season there is an excess capacity of accommodation. Recently, some surplus accommodation has been taken out of the market and reconverted into private homes, but not enough to increase the competitiveness of the remaining facilities. New developments are rare: not since the late 1930s has a new hotel been erected, although some extentions to exisiting establishments have been built.

Fierce competition has landed the tourism sector in severe difficulties. The economic potential for recovery does not exist within the sector itself. Seen in a wider perspective, the economy of the island cannot be expected to be particularly supportive in regard to the recovery of the tourism sector, even though around 20 per cent of the working population is dependent on tourism[111]. The unemployment rate on the island (claimant unemployment rates) is 12.2 per cent, compared to the UK average of 8.9 per cent[112].

---

111   Isle of Wight Tourism and Southern Tourist Board: Isle of Wight tourism strategy, April 1994

112   As at January 1995. Source: Central Statistical Office: Regional trends, 1995 edition, 1995

In the UK, only one other county suffers from an unemployment rate that is higher than on the Isle of Wight. Average salaries are only 5 per cent lower than the UK standard, but in 1991 the per capita GNP was calculated to amount to 70.7 per cent of the British average. This situation has worsened since 1981, when the Isle of Wight GNP amounted to 75.9 per cent of the UK average[113].

The slowing down of the Isle of Wight economy over the last decade has resulted in continual applications for EU regional development status. This designation has, however, never been given to the island - a matter of increasing concern as no other relevant regional development programmes are available to the islanders and their businesses. The "Isle of Wight Tourism Strategy" can be seen as an isolated attempt to pool slender resources into a joint effort: the strategy is, however, not part of a comprehensive development strategy encompassing all sectors of the economy.

To conclude, it may be regarded as an established fact that tourism has been a very important means of income and employment on the Isle of Wight. The islanders are, however, aware that their ability to secure an income from this source is declining dramatically. Holiday-makers changed preferences constitute only one reason for the decline; the structure of the industry is another important factor explaining why tourism is stuck in a downward spiral.

The ongoing debate on this issue is predominantly concerned with defensive measures to hold onto what is still left and eventually to launch into new markets.

From an environmental point of view, the following observations are of extreme importance:

- The issues of economic crisis in general and the decline of tourism in particular are regarded as being so important that they overrule environmental challenges.

- Although tourism volumes have dropped, they are still considerable. That tourism has an impact on the environment is certain. Tourism is, however, concentrated in the Sandown/ Shanklin, Ventnor and Ryde areas, thus presenting some opportunities for environmental planning and control.

---

113   Ibid.

- The holiday-makers are predominantly British middle/low income families. This market segment demonstrates less environmental awareness and concern than higher-income groups and other nationalities (particularly Germans and Dutch). Therefore, this market is less likely to exert any pressure to improve environmental standards on the Isle of Wight than is the case with destinations with higher socio-economic groupings of tourists.

- A large proportion of the tourism facilities is in the hands of people who do not depend entirely on incomes from tourism. This peculiarity is important in terms of being able to remain flexible and in terms of surviving in times of slow business conditions. Proprietors who are part of this type of industrial structure will tend to limit their investments and tend not to ensure a continued professionalization of their operations. It seems probable that this will negativly affect the readiness to be proactive when it comes to measures concerned with the environment.

4.3. The nature and extent of environmental constraints

This section identifies environmental opportunities and constraints. In this section it is assumed that tourism affects the environment, and that at the same time tourism relies on environmental resources. The sources of information used to describe these phenomena are interviews with key persons and material provided by the authorities on the advantages and problems that the island faces in relation to tourism.

Information on resource availability will be compared to data on vulnerability, when such data are available. The following themes will be covered in the analysis:

- Changes in landscapes and towns
- Fresh water supply
- Waste water treatment
- Noise
- Solid waste treatment
- Energy supply.

4.3.1. Changes in landscapes and towns

Beaches and landscapes. The Isle of Wight exhibits an unusual diversity of geological attractions within a comparatively small area: sedimentary origins, very pressed and folded, with surfaces eroded to produce the type of geological features which can be observed on the surface today. The "trademarks" of the Isle of Wight are the impressive chalk and gault undercliffs, particularly on the southern coasts. Apart from these distinctive features, the island includes woodlands, downlands, chines, rivers, sandcoasts and wetlands - forming the basis for a variety of flora and fauna, including one of England's last remaining colonies of red squirrels.

Every year natural forces erode and take away considerable parts of the vulnerable coastlines. Compared to this loss of landscape values, the population and the authorities consider the activities of tourists as having only limited importance.

Tourism developments are particularly concentrated at a few coastal locations, and hardly any expansion has taken place outside these areas. In recent years, however, a number of golf courses have been established, some of them close to prominent coastlines. The countryside has also been invaded by other leisure activities which directly or indirectly affect their appearance. For instance, the growing popularity of horse riding has resulted in the partly uncontrolled establishment of stables in the countryside.

The island provides very good opportunities for mountainbiking, hang-gliding, climbing and other "extreme" sports. The authorities are not particularly concerned that this might cause landscape erosion. Rather, they tend to see these natural features as opportunities which will compensate for some of the decline of tourism. For instance, the launching of two large mountain-biking events has been warmly supported[114]. German aviation enthusiasts are also allowed to perform private flying and gliding on the Isle of Wight, though they are prohibited from doing so in their home country.

As in other parts of Britain, the Isle of Wight countryside is open to foot passage on trails and small roads. More than 800 kilometres are available, and the paths are normally signposted and well marketed. Too heavy use of the most sensitive areas is discouraged through the low standards of the supporting facilities.

---

114   Competitive mountain biking is reported to be the fastest growing UK sport. Croall, Jonathan: Preserve or destroy. Tourism and the environment, Gulbenkian Foundation, London 1995

The built-up environment. The major part of the tourist accommodation capacity consists of Victorian villas and manor houses located along the coast, but predominantly in Sandown, Shanklin, Ventnor and Ryde. Many houses are listed. The open structure with gardens is retained, in spite of the fact that many hotels have built extensions and car parks. The towns retain their Victorian atmosphere which may be regarded as an asset, although the locals do not tend to advance this opinion. The originality of style tends to be overruled by a first impression of neglect of the public infrastructure and a lack of appropriate maintenance of private property. Many hotels are not fitted with en-suite bathroom facilities, and thus they do not meet basic modern standards. One type of tourist accommodation which is causing particular concern are the sites for fixed caravans and chalets. The sites provide cheap accommodation, but most often they are visually unattractive.

Market surveys indicate that the image of the island is highly dependent on its scenery and villages. A TV campaign has succeeded in enhancing the image of the island as a "beautiful" and "unspoilt" place[115]. These surveys do not include other and more specific indicators related to the environment.

4.3.2. Fresh water supply

Under normal circumstances, the Isle of Wight contains enough fresh water reserves to cover requirements. Summer droughts have been problematic, however, and a pipeline to the mainland has been installed in order to supply the island in critical situations. Generally, the water supply is not considered to be a constraint on tourism development on the island. Water meters have only recently been installed in private homes (including many guest houses and other tourist facilities).

There are no reports on the impact of agricultural nutrients and pesticides on the ground water reserves. This issue is not mentioned in local planning documents, where other concerns related to agriculture dominate, for instance the preservation of the best soil for agricultural purposes[116]. The draft unitary development plan [117]touches upon the need

---

115   PA Consultants: Isle of Wight visitor survey, May 1994; and MSS Marketing Research: Isle of Wight pre and post omnibus study 1994/95

116   Conrad, Jobst: Nitrate pollution and politics. Great Britain, the Federal Republic of Germany and the Netherlands, Avebury, Aldershot, 1990 concludes that in Britain the formalization of nitrate policies is at a low level, and that in comparison to the other countries public pressure does not yet exist. The issue is included in "Sustainable development. The UK strategy"

to assess the potential risks of polluting aquifers and introduces zoning options.

4.3.3. Waste water treatment

The Isle of Wight is located at the mouth of the river Solent, which takes (in most cases treated) waste water from large cities such as Southampton and Portsmouth to the English Channel. The waste generated by residents and tourists is also discharged into the marine environment around the island. Waste water is only given a preliminary or primary treatment. There are no plants undertaking a second or further treatment of waste water on the island[118].

In spite of the fact that the waters north of the island are "controlled waters"[119], some holiday-makers regard the environmental standard of the sea and coast as too low. During the important annual yachting events at Cowes, participants have claimed that the sea is unacceptably dirty. The south coast has not caused the same type of complaints, although seaborne waste and some algae are polluting the coasts.

Southern Water Services, a private company which has taken over sewage treatment as part of the privatization process, is considering a solution to the problems on the north coast involving the construction of a pipeline conducting the sewage down to the south coast and out beyond the three kilometre limit of "controlled water". It can then be discharged without having to meet quality standards. Southern Water considers further treatment of the sewage before finally discharging it - thus bringing the waste water up to a standard that complies with EU recommendations - to be beyond the pockets of the users of the sewage system, and therefore this type of investment is given lower priority than other localities and types of investments[120].

(1994). The policy advocated contains three elements: 1. Complying with the EU CAP (Common Agricultural Policy) with its set-aside schemes, 2. Zoning of particularly vulnerable areas and 3. Voluntary schemes for farmers.

117   Isle of Wight Council: Unitary development plan. Consultation draft, February 1996

118   Isle of Wight Council: Unitary development plan. Consultation draft, February 1996

119   According to National Rivers Authority standards

120   Southern Water Services: Conservation and the environment. The Report for 1994/1995

There are no Blue Flag designations on the coast of the Isle of Wight, but the council claims that this is because it does not want to invest in the required beach facilities.

4.3.4. Noise

There are no particular noise difficulties reported on the Isle of Wight. The island has an image of being quiet - for better or for worse. Noise from a high level of car traffic seems to be accepted by the tourists, and the nuisances mentioned are predominantly those concerned with congestion and parking. In spite of the fact that some noisy sports activities take place, they are not regarded as severe in regard to the environment.

4.3.5. Solid waste treatment

The volume of tourism has a significant effect on the production of solid waste. As most accommodation establishments are very small, the Waste Regulation Authorities (Isle of Wight Council) treat them as private households. Larger hotels enter a separate scheme, where waste glass, for example, is collected by the authorities for recycling.

Another feature of recycling consists of bottle banks in all urban settlements and collection schemes for aluminium soft drink cans. In the summer, containers are placed on the beaches and in car parks in order to increase the recycling of these items. The scheme was established in co-operation with a charity organization so as to ensure a comprehensive collection of aluminium cans and in addition to provide the organization with a source of funds.

The County Council has set an objective of recycling 25 per cent of solid waste. This objective has been more than fulfilled, because the burning of waste (processed to fuel pellets) in a power station is regarded as recycling. Experiments with the composting of garden and park waste is encouraged, and bins for this purpose are given away to private house owners. Nonetheless, over half of the solid waste is placed in land fills.

In 1996 waste treatment is about to be privatized. As part of the preparations, recycling projects which are not considered profitable are to be taken out of the recycling programme.

4.3.6. Energy supply

Electricity is provided by private enterprises. Recycled fuel pellets fed into electricity production account for a minor part of energy consumption ("the street lighting twice over")[121].

There is no district heating on the island. Hotels and other tourist establishments use central heating, or are heated by means of electric or gas radiators. Central heating is considered a special advantage: hotels with central heating systems draw attention to this fact in their marketing material.

Solar heating of swimming pools can be observed, but the use of renewable energy is rare. There are no wind generation plants in spite of good wind reserves, and no biogas, although agriculture on the island is extensive.

The tourism sector has no particular tradition of saving energy. Insulation of buildings and measures to ensure the efficient use of energy are not often brought into play. The reason given to explain this is the impossibility of paying the first investment, even if the pay-back period is proven to be short.

The island has a small airport, but the majority of transport to the island is via the ferries. A ferry is normally considered an energy efficient means of transportation, although catamarans compromise this image. Still more tourists bring their own car in order to be mobile during their stay on the island. Also coach tours tend to cause tourists to move about more than was the case in earlier days.

The amount of energy used for transportation purposes has risen, but the Isle of Wight may still be claimed to be a tourist destination necessitating only a moderate consumption of energy, as the tourists are mostly British and predominantly come from southern England.

The public transport system has been privatized, but a fairly extensive network is available. Summer routes are provided to popular locations. Public transport is considered an expensive mode of transportation on the island, and it cannot compete

---

121   Isle of Wight County Council: Electricity for the Island. A County Council Initiative, leaflet, n.d.

with private cars.

Cycling is popular on the island, but this activity takes place particularly on small roads. Only a few dedicated bicycle trails are available, although the conversion of old rail tracks into cycleways is on the agenda.

4.3.7. Conclusions

The dominant environmental problems on the Isle of Wight - in relation to tourism - are the following:

- The lack of appropriate waste water treatment. There is concern that this issue will cause a deterioration of the image of the island, particularly among new and more affluent segments of holiday-makers (those preferring activities such as yachting, surfing, angling, etc).

- The structure of the tourism industry with very small enterprises is not an environmental problem as such. However, the dynamics of degradation are assisted by the fragmented pattern of ownership and the lack of any inclination towards professionalism. This is an issue which severely affects the overall opportunities for future tourism development. The fact that water and energy is not used efficiently may be considered a side-effect of neglecting one's premises.

- The natural environment is a recognized, much appreciated and still abundant resource on the Isle of Wight. If an increase in "extreme sports" takes place, this may give rise to concern as to how to limit the damage caused in the natural environment. Although there is pressure to attract more events and more individual sportsmen, the authorities have not envisaged any controlling mechanisms to deal with the adverse consequences that might arise.

- Privatized enterprises in waste treatment, public transport, water supply, etc., operate on the basis of financial objectives only. Long-term sustainability has not been particularly integrated into their strategies. Hardly any motivation exists for entering into co-operative relations with the authorities and the tourism industry in order to increase the sustainable use of scarce resources.

The environmental situation on the Isle of Wight cannot be considered dire. But in the longer-term there are significant threats. Rising environmental awareness among holiday-makers on the one hand, and a deteriorating and inactive tourism sector on the other, is a dangerous combination.

4.4. The environmental regulation system

4.4.1. Authorities

The Department of the Environment is the central governmental department with overall responsibility for implementing the Government's environmental policy. Another important department when it comes to protection issues is the Department of National Heritage. Both departments have extensive powers to prepare detailed legislation within the framework of the statutes passed by the Government and to up-date legislation in order to accommodate, for instance, EU developments and changing standards. They delegate most of the day-to-day decision making to various regulatory bodies, but hear appeals against their decisions and control their finances. To a certain degree, the delegation of powers in environmental affairs takes place at the regional and local levels.

The Isle of Wight is an independent county with a county council. Until recently, the island was also divided into two district councils, South Wight and Medina. However, the island was among the first regions to adopt what is called a "unitary authority", combining the responsibilities of the districts and the council into one organization. This development has been advocated by the national government in order to increase the efficiency of local administration. The amalgamation was finalized in 1995.

The County Council does not have an independent tax base. Funds from the Treasury are, however, allocated for purposes such as infrastructure, leisure facilities, cultural activities, etc., all areas under the administration of the Council. Waste management is also a county responsibility. The activities and administration procedures of the Council must comply with national policies and regulations. Strategies and plans are subject to approval by the national authorities.

A number of other statutory bodies, which are defined by sector rather than region, are very important agents in the regulation of the environment in the United Kingdom:

Her Majesty's Inspectorate of Pollution is a division of the Department of the Environment set up to provide a coherent approach to pollution control. Among its responsibilities are research into, the publishing of guidelines for, and the control of emissions from heavily polluting processes. The inspectorate is in charge of monitoring the operations of local waste authorities.

The National Rivers Authority (NRA) is an independent agency set up in 1989 to deal with a variety of matters related to water. Its main pollution-related functions are the issue of discharge permissions, which limit the release of polluting substances into rivers, lakes and other waters. The agency is also in charge of water quality and the prosecution of unauthorized polluters[122].

The 1989 Act transferred water supply and sewage functions to privately owned water and sewage companies. The trade effluents discharged into sewers is taken care of by the private sewage companies subsequent to their having obtained the necessary consent from the NRA to discharge the treated output from sewage works into rivers and seas[123].

According to the Water Resources Act of 1991, the National Rivers Authority also has duties and powers which include the recreational use of rivers. Licences for anglers and boat owners are issued by the NRA.

Some other statutory bodies sponsored by the Department of the Environment are important to sustainability in tourism:

The Forestry Commission is responsible for advising on and implementing the forest policy, and the Commission controls state-owned forests.

The Countryside Commission is the Government's principal advisor on the conservation of the English countryside. It does not have ownership of land or facilities but works with others to achieve three broad aims: "To conserve and enhance the scenic, natural and historic qualities of the whole of the countryside; to secure and extend opportunities for people to enjoy and use the countryside for open-air recreation; and to promote

---

122   Heaton, Andrew: Conservation and the National Rivers Authority in Goldsmith, F.B. and A. Warren (eds): Conservation in progress, Wiley and Sons, Chichester, 1995, pp 301-320

123   Symes, Tom and Victoria Phillips: England and Wales in Beadley, Mark (ed): Environmental liabilities and regulation in Europe, International Business Publishing, The Hague, 1992

understanding of the countryside, its life and work, agriculture and forestry and the economic and social needs of the countryside"[124].

The Countryside Commission is responsible for the designation of Areas of Outstanding Natural Beauty (see below).

English Nature is responsible for advising national and local governments on nature conservation and for promoting wildlife and natural features. This includes the establishment, maintenance and management of Natural Nature Reserves and the promotion of Sites of Special Scientific Interest.

The Rural Development Commission advises the Government on the economic and social development of rural areas. The diversification of agricultural holdings into tourism activities is within the remit of the Commission.

The Department of National Heritage supports the following bodies:

The British Tourist Authority and The English Tourist Board aim to maximize tourist arrivals from overseas and to advise Government and public bodies on matters affecting incoming tourism to Britain. The English Tourist Board has actively supported and co-funded a number of activities in general and also some activities on a regional basis which are concerned with the development of sustainable tourism, but its policy has increasingly moved towards a "hands-off" approach[125].

The regional tourist boards are non-statutory bodies, often - as it is the case on the Isle of Wight - operating on a purely commercial basis.

From the description above, it becomes obvious that in the UK a number of statutory and non-statutory bodies and agents are active in the environmental arena. This has been considered inefficient, and in 1996 the Environment Agency was established as a division of the Department of the Environment to deal with environmental protection in a more efficient way.

---

124   Adapted from: Environment Committee: The environmental impact of leisure activities, House of Commons, London, 1995

125   Croall, Jonathan: Preserve or destroy. Tourism and the environment, Gulbenkian Foundation, London 1995

108

Private bodies

For more than a decade, the general trend in the UK has been towards privatization of formerly publicly controlled facilities and supply systems. Accordingly, a number of private contractors have become active partners in the decision-making process and in the implementation of environmental policies. On the Isle of Wight, privatization has taken place within the following sectors, all of vital importance to the environment:

- water supply
- waste water treatment
- energy supplies
- public transport.

Privatization of solid waste treatment is expected to be carried through in the near future.

4.4.2. Regulation by laws, plans and standards

Parks and nature reserves. The preservation of natural heritage is an important issue in the UK, and for quite some time now, legislation has been in place to pursue this objective and at the same time ensure public access to the countryside. The Town and Country Act of 1947 stipulated the obligatory preparation of the first Development Plans covering the entire country, and in 1949 the National Parks and the Access to the Countryside Act opened up possibilities for designating valuable landscapes for future protection[126].

Considerable areas have been designated as "Areas of Outstanding Natural Beauty" (A-ONBs). In the Isle of Wight alone, 189 square kilometres, representing more than half of the total area of the island, have been so designated. Protection of the AONBs lies in the hands of the county council, which is expected to include protection issues in its structure and local plans.

Another means of protection is the designation of selected coastlines as "heritage coasts". The spectacular south coast of the Isle of Wight has been designated in this

---

126   Cherry, Gordon E.: Changing social attitudes towards leisure and the countryside in Britain, 1890-1990 in Glyptis, Sue (ed): Leisure and the environment, Belhaven, London 1993, pp 22-32

way. The same type of planning is expected for the heritage coasts as for AONBs. Designations as "areas of outstanding natural beauty" and "heritage coasts" are non-statutory. However, the mere designation raises awareness of the qualities of the area among its inhabitants and in particular among the numerous NGOs in charge of nature. These designations, in combination with the activities of the conservation lobby, have an effect on the authorities who will attempt to keep new developments out of the vulnerable areas, and to assist land owners and inform them as to how to handle modernization, extensions, fencing, advertising, etc. In addition, it has become more and more necessary to provide facilities such as car parks for visitors, a matter which must also be included in the plans[127]. On the other hand, developers continually challenge the designations, although this type of pressure has been very frequent on the Isle of Wight.

On the Isle of Wight, the main issue has been to ensure public access to privately owned areas. Negotiations with land owners to create sufficient possibilities of passage by means of footpaths and bridleways resulted in a substantial signposted and mapped network being made available to the population as well as to the tourists.

Sites of Special Scientific Interest (SSSIs) enjoy special protection by the government. Being particularly interesting in terms of geology and biology, the Isle of Wight has 43 SSSIs, but each of these areas is small. Two wild bird sanctuary orders made in the 1950s still remain in force.

The land remains in private ownership, and the owners or occupiers are prohibited from carrying out specified potentially damaging activities, for instance building or drainage operations, without giving four months notice. On receiving such notice, the national authorities may consent to the operation in question or negotiate terms with the owners, but they have no power to actually prevent such activities from being carried out. There is a significant penalty for owners or occupiers who are in breach of these provisions, i.e. the maximum fine is fixed at £1,000.

Management agreements along with subsidies made available to the owners ensure that the areas are protected as prescribed. Accordingly, the mode of regulation applied to these specific areas is the combination of a designation procedure and economic incentives. The penalties charged for breaking agreements and regulations are not

---

127   Isle of Wight Council: Unitary development plan. Consultation draft, February 1996 and The
        Isle of Wight AONB Joint Advisory Committee: Isle of Wight AONB Management Plan
        Summary, August 1994

adequate enough to prevent damages. Adams[128] shows that, over the years, SSSIs in Britain have suffered from considerable losses and damage caused by excessive agricultural and forestry practices and residential developments. The amount of funds available from the Treasury to cover the costs of management contracts have been cut, and will in future probably not be sufficient to ensure continued protection and care along the same lines as previously.

Land-use plans. The UK planning system plays an important part in environmental regulation. Planning is the chosen method for resolving potential environmental conflicts. National planning priorities are set out in so-called Planning Policy Guidelines (PPG), of which a number are relevant to tourism:

- PPG 2 : Green Belts
- PPG 9 : Nature Conservation
- PPG 17 : Sport and Recreation
- PPG 20 : Planning the Coast
- PPG 21 : Tourism

The PPGs outline principles and criteria of development. The PPG on tourism[129], for instance, includes fundamental guidelines governing the location of new hotels, modernization and extensions, and outlining how to undertake local consultation and how to handle open-air advertisements.

The *structural plans* of the regional authorities are supposed to reflect the relevant departmental guidelines. Below the regional level, *local plans* must be prepared by the district councils.

Following the establishment of the unitary authority on the Isle of Wight, a new "unitary development plan" is being prepared, and a commentary version of it was published in the spring of 1996. This plan includes a structural plan as well as local plans and maps indicating in detail what use has been suggested for the land in the area. Although the

---

128   Adams, W.M.: Places for Nature: Protected Areas in British Nature Conservation in Gold-smith, F.B. and Warren A.(eds): Conservation in Progress, Wiley and Sons, Chichester, 1995, pp 185-208

129   Department of the Environment: Planning policy guidance: Tourism, PPG 21, November 1992

development plan reflects the problems and potentials of tourism on the island, it is predominantly a land-use plan which aims at the regulation of the built-up environment. In addition, it allocates land for proposed future infrastructural investments and other developments.

Even with these limitations, proactive environmental regulation measures might still be included in the development plan. The Isle of Wight proposal introduces attempts to ensure environmental awareness within the field of tourism and leisure. For instance, new developments are primarily to take place in or in connection with an existing resort, so as to ensure the protection of landscapes. The plan also advocates a more pronounced emphasis on public transport and the provision of cycleways so as to enhance sustainable transportation. Applications for leisure and sports facilities for residents and tourists will normally be approved if they are located within or adjacent to existing settlements. New establishments in protected areas will be given low priority.

Generally speaking, the development plan is a "passive" set of guidelines. The council does not possess funds or other measures to ensure rapid implementation of some of the proposed strategies and investments. The realization of the development plan depends on the private sector - thus the council faces the difficult task of preparing the plan in such a way as to make it appeal to investors. Over the last few years, applications for major planning permissions have been very rare thanks to the depressed economic state of the tourism sector of the island.

There is a consultation period of nearly two years before final approval can be given. This is to ensure that the local population, the land owners, the potential investors and the Department of the Environment are in agreement about the plan. Considerable alterations of the existing proposal are expected before the final Isle of Wight development plan can be published. A coastal management plan is also in the making.

EIA (Environmental Impact Assessment). In Britain, the EU Directive 85/337 was introduced into national legislation via the Town and Country Planning Regulations 1988 (SI 1988/1199). This meant that submitting an Environmental Statement became part of the normal application procedure to obtain planning consent for a range of specified developments[130]. Because of the very limited investment activities in tourism on the Isle of Wight, no environmental assessments have ever taken place.

---

130   Ravenscroft, Neil: The environmental impact of recreation and tourism development: A review in European Environment, vol 2, part 2, 1992; and Glasson, John et al: Introduction to environmental impact assessment, UCL Press, London, 1994

Energy policy. The Department of Energy lacks a comprehensive formal articulation of policy themes, a matter which has been the subject of criticism from, for instance, the International Energy Agency and the European Commission[131]. The 1990 White Paper on the Environment does include energy related actions, and the implementation of energy efficiency and energy saving programmes have also been included[132]. Regional authorities have limited influence on energy policy.

Since 1990, environmental policies have been given higher priority by the Government, and greater emphasis has been put on the integration of environmental considerations into economic policy decisions. The preamble of the environmental strategy of the government contains an indication of the role of regulation: "The traditional way of reducing environmental damage has been to impose regulatory requirements, for example, the control of emissions by the pollution control authorities, or of land development through the planning system. But regulation may not always be the best way of achieving objectives either from an environmental or an economic point of view. Regulation imposes hidden costs which can lead to inefficiency and waste. The Government's general policy is to reduce and simplify regulations wherever appropriate". [133]

Accordingly, the Government encourages the local authorities to engage themselves in other modes of promoting sustainable tourism and leisure. Participation in Agenda 21 is mentioned, thus introducing a "softer" and more flexible approach.

4.4.3. Regulation by means of financial instruments

The privatization process. For more than a decade, the political climate has favoured a transfer of environmental bodies and organizations to private ownership. A comprehensive privatization process has taken place within the water and energy supply system and within the waste water treatment and public transport systems. The

---

131   Boehmer-Christiansen, Sonja and Jim Skea: Acid politics: Environmental and energy policies in Britain and Germany, Belhaven Press, London and New York, 1991 and Collier, Ute: Energy and Environment in the European Union. The challenge of integration, Avebury, Aldershot, 1994

132   Therivel, Riki et al: Strategic environmental assessment, Earthscan Publications, London, 1992; and UK Government: Sustainable development. The UK strategy, HMSO, London, 1994

133   UK Government: Sustainable development. The UK strategy, HMSO, London, 1994, p 34

Government claims that private control will increase efficiency and eventually provide consumers with cheaper services, particularly if competition is introduced parallel to privatization.

There is a strong belief among a majority of the population that market forces will ensure higher efficiency, and perhaps lower prices - and tax cuts - as well. Consumers will vote through their purchasing behaviour. Enterprises will adjust themselves to consumer demands by raising standards and improving quality.

When it comes to environmental issues, the implementation of the ultimative privatization strategy has been opposed by the EU. The British Government had intended to let private companies be responsible for supplying both drinking water and sewage disposal, and also for regulatory functions such as pollution control, including discharges to rivers. EU directives did, however, require authorization by a "competent authority", and the question was raised of whether a private company primarily answerable to its shareholders could act as a "competent authority".[134]

Within the framework of EU regulations, a dominant mode of administration consists in letting the market forces work as freely as possible, and setting up only the necessary standards of protection. For instance, fixed standards are maintained when granting consents authorizing the discharge of certain substances into waters, consents which may impose a variety of conditions. Recently, a system of charges for discharging certain substances has been brought in, thus implementing the "polluter pays" principle. Where discharge consents are exceeded, the National Rivers Authority can prosecute the polluter. This is happening more and more frequently with sewage plants, industries and agricultural holdings.

The price mechanisms that have been introduced have had some positive influence on environmental behaviour. For instance, on the Isle of Wight (as in the rest of the country) only industrial water consumption used to be metered. After the introduction of privatization, domestic water meters were also installed in a number of tourism accommodation units, and this action has been reported to encourage savings.

On the other hand, fares on public transport have become more expensive since privatization, and tourists as well as the local population do not feel particularly inclined

---

134   Haig, Nigel: EEC. Policy and implementation in European Environmental Handbook, 1991, pp 86-87

to use the facilities. Services to remote villages and areas have been cut as well.

Plans to privatize solid waste management have already affected the recycling programme on the Isle of Wight. Plastic is no longer recycled because that is not financially viable. Funds for awareness campaigns among tourism enterprises are available, but money can only be spent on condition that a financially positive impact can be expected.

Investment incentives. There are no public (governmental or regional) programmes or funds dedicated to the promotion of energy or water saving measures, or aiming to reduce waste, etc. in the tourism sector.

The national environmental strategy[135] does allocate funds for strategically important activities, for example for basic research into environmental issues and for awareness programmes and auditing schemes. But the funds are not directly available to ensure private investment in more sustainable types of tourism. Accordingly, neither private enterprises nor public authorities are in a position to apply for government funds towards the implementation of sustainable strategies.

The Rural Development Commission has supported some projects on the island, and indirectly the Training and Enterprise Council provides enterprises with financial assistance. There are, however, only rather modest links to environmental sustainability. So-called "Landscape Improvement Grants" are available to land owners and other agents in Areas of Outstanding Natural Beauty/Heritage Coasts. Support is given to projects concerned with such activities as, e.g. local landscaping, eyesore removal, habitat creation or management, access improvements, historic parks and gardens, improving business and tourist sites. The grants are normally very limited - a maximum of £2,000. Agricultural policies also indirectly support the sustainable tourism issue: grants have been given to agricultural holdings in order to enable them to diversify and to encourage the establishment of facilities for rural tourism complying with the general "ideology of countryside leisure"[136].

The implementation and funding of sustainable strategies rely very heavily on private initiatives or funds accounted for in the budgets of the Council. The availability of these

135   UK Government: Sustainable development: The UK strategy, HMSO, London, 1994

136   Clark, Gordon et al: Leisure landscapes. Leisure, culture and the English countryside. Challenges and conflicts, Lancaster University, May 1994

types of development fund is claimed to be extremely restricted on the Isle of Wight.

Fees and tourist taxes. Fees are used on several occasions as part of the regulatory system. For instance, anglers and boat owners have to pay for their right to use natural resources for their sports. To obtain planning permission, developers must pay fees, but revenues only cover administrative costs, and do not contribute towards any type of communal environmental investment.

Tourism enterprises and tourists do not pay any general taxes (levies) which could be allocated for environmental purposes. Revenues are, however, created by means of car parking charges and hiring out deck chairs on beaches, etc. Visitors to sites owned by the National Trust are to an increasing extent asked to contribute to management costs, and so a voluntary green tax has been indirectly introduced levied from those who use the sites[137].

Voluntary activities are very important as part of enhancing the natural environment in terms of interpretation and the provision of infrastructure. The National Trust plays a major role in the activities on the Isle of Wight, owning and controlling large areas of great importance to the environment. Tax exemption measures enable voluntary bodies to acquire land free of any charges, or at greatly reduced costs, thus indirectly subsidizing this mode of organizing environmental preservation. Corporate funding for voluntary environmental conservation has grown, in part to enhance the "green image" of the enterprises.

Management contracts. As mentioned above, the designation of Sites of Special Scientific Interest may be safeguarded through the drawing up of management contracts between the national authorities and the occupiers. The annual or lump sum payments are intended to compensate for any additional costs incurred in connection with the maintenance of these areas, or they may be seen as a compensation for the loss of alternative income from the land. However, the system of SSSIs has not been particularly successful in terms of protection; many sites have been destroyed or are threatened, as financial compensation is insufficient, and no other means of regulation are available.[138]

---

137   English Tourist Board: Tourism and the environment. Maintaining the balance, London, 1991

138   Adams, W.M.: Places for Nature: Protected Areas in British Nature Conservation in Gold-smith, F.B and Warren A.(eds): Conservation in Progress, Wiley and Sons, Chichester, 1995, pp 185-208

Private funds. Some funds are available which might assist development towards sustainable tourism. One example is the lottery-funded "Millennium Fund", which will in the course of the coming years make funds available to co-finance large and smaller projects to do with visitor attractions related to heritage or nature. So far, the bulk of the funds awarded has gone to environmental, community, science and technology and major landmark projects.

The National Heritage Memorial Fund is also available to schemes and projects which preserve and enhance specific natural resources of local, regional or national importance.

The principles promoted by the Government aim to enhance the market mechanisms for the benefit of the environment. The Government is examining the possibilities of introducing tradeable permits, levies, etc., but the selection and implementation of financial instruments is still in a very preliminary phase.[139]

4.4.4. Collaborative and behavioural measures

The environmental protection lobby in Britain is extremely powerful, and it organizes large sections of the population who support the conservation of the built and natural environments. To a certain extent the influence of the lobby counterbalances the lack of regulatory powers in the hands of the authorities.[140] One of the largest organizations - the National Trust - purchases and also inherits land in order to ensure comprehensive protection. On the Isle of Wight, the National Trust owns 1,600 ha of countryside and 16 miles of coastline, and the organization is widely respected for its efforts to provide public access and to ensure a sustainable use of these areas. However, the protection lobby mainly takes defensive action, and directs its efforts towards very specific geographical areas or selected natural resources, habitats or species.

Collaboration on the other side of the table, i.e. within the tourism industry, is organized by eight trade associations for hoteliers and suppliers of attractions. The All Island Tourist Association is an umbrella organization established only recently in order to

---

139   UK Government: Sustainable development. The UK strategy, HMSO, London, 1994

140   Gittins, John: Community involvement in environment and recreation in Glyptis, Sue (ed): Leisure and the environment, Belhaven, London, 1993, pp 183-192

ensure the co-ordination of trade activities. The mission of the All Island Tourist Association mainly consists of ensuring that marketing initiatives are efficiently carried out. The association does, however, also participate in a new "Tourism Partnership", which is made up of six county councillors and six commercial representatives. The main task of the Tourism Partnership is to act as a consultative body to the County Council, and to manage the contract between the marketing organization of Isle of Wight Tourism and Southern Tourism.

None of these business-dominated organizations have been particularly keen on addressing the issue of sustainability. Their main objective is to ensure efficient marketing, and to lobby for the establishment of new attractions. An application in pursuance of the latter objective has been presented to the Millennium Fund with a view to establishing a new visitor centre in Ventnor themed around flora, fauna and geology.

The Isle of Wight Tourism Strategy, which was devised by Isle of Wight Tourism and Southern Tourism in collaboration with the County Council, the district councils, commercial partners, Wight Training and Enterprise and Rural Development Commission, includes a general objective and a number of actions to promote sustainable tourism. The objective, which has been given high priority, reads as follows:

> To instigate and support initiatives which aim to safeguard the island's natural resources and enhance its general appearance in resort areas.

The actions designed to achieve this objective are the following:

(i)   The island could be marketed more strongly as a "green tourism product" in promotional print. This image will appeal especially to short break takers and the wealthy over 55s, two potential markets for the island.

(ii)   Seafront refurbishments should be encouraged... Ideally, all of the island's seafronts should be the subject of strategies which aim to create a quality ambience.

(iii)   Holiday-makers' perception of beach and water quality is important to their choice of holiday destination. Whilst the understanding of the criteria underlying the Blue Flag designation might be limited, it has, nevertheless, acquired a status which is assuming still greater importance in the eyes of the public. The island's resorts should be working towards Blue Flag accreditation within the next three years. There is an important role here for local authorities in renewing and improving beach facilities. Pressure also needs to be placed on Southern Water and the National Rivers Authority to ensure the highest possible levels of treatment in relation to new and existing outfalls. Efforts are also required to ensure that the Solent retains its EU estuarial status, so that the associated requirements for second as well as first stage treatment of sewage is maintained.

(iv)   ... The potential of local environmental trusts is currently being explored.

(v)   Local authority tree planting/landscaping grants should be made available and promoted to holiday caravan park operators.

(vi)   Support should be maintained for the Area of Outstanding Natural Beauty Project and the island's Countryside Management Service which helps to maintain many of the island's more fragile environments and to manage visitor pressures. This includes the enhancement of Heritage Coast paths. However, greater representation by the tourism industry on management committees/groups should be sought.[141]

As can be seen from the list of actions proposed, the tourism organizations have only limited powers to actually change the course of tourism and make it move in a more sustainable direction. The majority of their efforts is put into making others take responsibility and into finding external funding for their actions. One exception is marketing, which is undertaken and financed by the industry itself. However, the lack of funds prevents the organization from launching campaigns in relevant foreign markets.

Initial discussions on the introduction of a "green label" for hotels have taken place, but

---

141   Isle of Wight Tourism and Southern Tourist Board: Isle of Wight Tourism Strategy, April 1994, pp 18-20

the issue has been postponed, partly because no formal and well-established nationwide system exists as yet and partly because it is believed that the hotel industry will not accept the idea. The existing inspectors of hotels for the English Tourist Board (the crown system) and the Automobile Association (the star system) do not concern themselves with environmental issues; they only refer to the available facilities.

Inclusive ferry fares have virtually become a pre-requisite for selling holidays to the island. The ferry companies are not involved in the environmental objectives and activities launched via the Isle of Wight Tourism Strategy. Nor does the largest ferry company, Wightlink, have a comprehensive environmental strategy of its own.

The Isle of Wight lacks other collaborative associates to promote and organize the business perspectives of sustainable tourism. Existing commercial tourism organizations are, however, not particularly optimistic when it comes to the opportunities for organizing a joint effort among tourism enterprises. Spokespeople refer to the fact that the individual tourism enterprise is most often small, and lacks resources and professionalism.

Tourism organizations stress that local authorities should take a "sympathetic and realistic approach to the wide range of new regulations and legislation emerging from the EU and Government Departments where there is local discretion. These have significant cost implications which potentially limit the resources for re-investment".[142] Accordingly, advancing green innovations by increasing the requirements to be fulfilled by the tourism industry, will not be met with understanding by tourism organizations and their member enterprises.

---

142   Isle of Wight Tourism and Southern Tourist Board: Isle of Wight Tourism Strategy, April 1994, p 20

4.4.5. Conclusions on environmental regulatory instruments

The above sections contained an analysiṡ of 1) regulation by means of laws and plans, 2) regulation via financial instruments, and 3) regulation by means of collaborative efforts and information. Taking an overall view encompassing all of these instruments, the following can be concluded:

- A very strong emphasis is placed on environmental regulation through market forces. The privatization of the operation of waste, water, energy, transport systems, etc. is the most evident expression of the belief in the benefits of a *free* market. Other more targeted types of financial instruments, such as green taxes, strategic investment subsidies, etc., are very infrequently used in Britain (and therefore on the Isle of Wight) as some of them are regarded as distorting the self-regulating potential of the market.

- In keeping with the emphasis placed on market forces, planning is a predominantly passive instrument, responsive only when challenged by land owners and investors. The Council Development Plan is a land-use plan, integrating the activities of other sectors only when they have spatial consequences. As they lack the formal powers to protect environmental resources from destruction through economic pressure, planners will often have to rely on the conservation lobbies, which are very powerful in Britain as well as on the Isle of Wight.

- Domination of the tourism industry by SMEs and the climate of liberal political influences tend to fragment the business and discourage co-operation. It is strongly believed that the backlog of investments existing in the private sector (in environmental improvements and in better standards generally) will be made up for if revenues can be created. "One of the most effective ways of achieving this is by creating a demand for existing and new products through imaginative marketing". [143]

- The trend on the Isle of Wight follows the national "wish to develop tourism opportunities in a way that will pre-empt conflict between major public interests. To this end, public and private sector bodies involved in, or

---

143   Isle of Wight Tourism and Southern Tourist Board: Isle of Wight Tourism Strategy, April 1994, p 20

affected by, tourism are engaged increasingly in the proliferating processes of negotiation and 'partnership' ... Within this framework, the statutory land use planning system is seen as having a distinct but residual role."[144]

This selection of regulatory models and instruments, combined with unfavourable market prospects on the Isle of Wight, results in a severe reluctance to bring environmental dimensions into tourism development. The Isle of Wight Tourism Strategy and the Council Development Plan both introduce the issue and set up visionary objectives. The lack of authority and of control of funds both imply that the process of implementation will probably be delayed or even abandoned.

Thanks to privatization, key sectors of environmental control, development and improvement (water, waste, energy, transport) are removed from immediate public influence. The Government intends to further couple this deregulation exercise with a major development in the use of financial instruments, saying it will consider a regulatory instrument only if a goal can not be achieved by a financial instrument.[145] Impacts on the environment resulting from privatization may in some respects be positive, if standards and requirements are set appropriately, or if environmental issues comply with economic interests.

However, it is not likely that contractors will proceed without substantial pressure, neither is it likely that they will involve themselves in sustainable tourism issues unless it may result in short- or long-term positive revenues.

4.5. Environmental innovations

4.5.1. The nature product

The Isle of Wight is recognized especially for the high quality of its coast and countryside. It benefits from the fact that an interest in conservation and heritage issues is widespread in the British population. The importance of the voluntary sector is well

---

144   Clark, Gordon et al: Leisure Landscapes. Leisure, Culture and the English Countryside: Challenges and Conflicts, CSEC, Lancaster University, 1994

145   Handler, Thomas: Regulating the European Environment, Chancery Law Publishing, 1994; and UK Government: Sustainable development: the UK Strategy, HMSO, 1994

recognized, the interrelationship between the interests of the private sector and the operations of nature protection organizations is better developed in Britain than in many other countries[146]. In addition, legislation which requires access to privately owned natural resources to be freely granted gives rise to innovative approaches to handling the issue of sustainability in regard to the use of the landscape.

Accordingly, in a British context, innovation within the field of sustainable tourism is very much associated with making nature *available* and *commodifying* supplementary services. Imaginative fundraising might also be considered an essential mode of innovation that enhances the environment.

4.5.2. The education market

The island appeals strongly to schools and colleges, as this one destination covers many National Curriculum subjects. In Britain - despite education cuts - schools are still obliged to include school trips in the educational calendar. A special marketing instrument, "a teachers' guide" presents the educational resources, accommodation and transport systems.

As a supplement, the Isle of Wight Training and Development Centre has been publishing teaching material for more than 20 years. Today, the list contains over 100 titles and ranges from simple worksheets to comprehensive multi-media packages which cover, and extend beyond, many areas of the curriculum for both very young schoolgoers and school leavers.

Commercial enterprises tend to lean on curriculum requirements as well, though they most often provide more entertaining elements, which are also attractive to the family holiday market. For instance, the Branstone Farm Studies Centre which is an open farm and Haseley Manor offering workshop experiences with arts and crafts.

4.5.3. The provision of trails

The "Public Rights of Way" principle is the legislative cornerstone of the provision of walking and riding trails on the Isle of Wight.

---

146   Gittins, John: Community involvement in environment and recreation in Glyptis, Sue (ed): Leisure and the environment, Belhaven, London, 1993, pp 183-192

148 miles of coastal trail are available, and additional much more extensive networks of smaller, but less heavily marketed trails, are generously offered to the public.

Waymarking is an essential part of trail development, and the design of signs and display boards attract much attention. The aesthetics of these items is considered of great importance to the overall impression of the standard of the trails and the types of experience with which visitors are provided.

In 1996, the Isle of Wight County Council will introduce a new type of guide, thus marketing the nature product more intensively to holiday-makers.

4.5.4. Codes of conduct

In connection with the establishment and marketing of the "Coastal Paths", the county surveyor pursues two sets of codes of conduct:[147]

The coastal code:

- Please do not damage salt marshes, sand dunes and "cliff tops" by trampling or by moving rocks;
- Make your visit instructive by planning field trips carefully with conservation in mind;
- Take photos, not live specimens;
- Always "backfill" holes when bait digging as these may represent a danger to others;
- Please do not collect live animals or seaweeds, leave them for others to enjoy;
- The coast is home to many animals and they may be destroyed by our careless actions.

The country code:
- Keep your dogs under close control
- Keep to the public paths across farmland

---

147   Source: Isle of Wight County Council: Coastal path leaflets

- Use gates and stiles to cross fences, hedges and walls
- Leave livestock, crops and machinery alone
- Take your litter home
- Help keep water clean
- Enjoy the countryside and respect its life and work
- Guard against all risks of fire
- Fasten all gates
- Protect wildlife, plants and trees
- Take special care on country roads
- Make no unnecessary noise.

4.5.4. Development of sporting events

To those who like an active holiday, the Isle of Wight offers many opportunities: cycling, fishing, golf, jet skiing, parascending, riding, sailing, snooker, swimming, walking, windsurfing, etc. The best known sport is sailing: Cowes Week at the end of July is widely marketed as the major event.

Based on the success of Cowes Week, the Isle of Wight tourism partners are intensifying their marketing of other sporting events, for instance regattas, yacht races, powerboat racing, cycling festivals, organized walks, angling competitions, windsurfing championships, etc. Commercial interest in the development of these events is considerable.

The expected positive impact associated with the environment mainly consists of a much welcomed spread of activities to shoulder season periods.

However, the organizers and authorities do not attempt to assess the environmental impacts of the sports and their side activities nor to improve their sustainability, as was for instance the case with the Lillehammer Winter Olympic Games. Rather, the island regards itself as a refuge for environmentally questionable activities, which are increasingly being restricted elsewhere.

5. Regimes of environmental regulation in tourism - summary, analysis and conclusions

5.1. Introduction

For many years, islands have caused concern among environmentalists and tourism analysts[148]. In terms of water catchment opportunities they are typically less favourably endowed than mainlands, and the options available for sustainable depositing of solid waste and waste water are fewer. Landscapes, the geological heritage and the flora and fauna are in many cases more vulnerable to extinction than they would be on larger surfaces. An island's environment has too little capacity to be able to counterbalance factors which disrupt its subtle equilibrium.

The pressure on the environment has increased over the past few decades. Many islands (particularly in warm waters) have become more attractive to tourists. Most often a development involving tourism is welcomed because alternative economic opportunities are rarely available. These days, regional development on islands hardly ever takes place without tourism as one or the only ingredient. The balancing of economic and environmental objectives is a crucial matter.

This study compares the environmental regulations of three European islands: Bornholm in Denmark, The Isle of Wight in the UK and Mallorca in Spain. For many decades, these islands have been experiencing considerable tourism inflows, although the composition of their markets and the speed and direction of developments vary.

---

148   Articles in Beller, W., P. d'Ayala and P. Hein (eds): Sustainable development and environmental management of small islands, Man and Biosphere Series, UNESCO, 1990 provide a comprehensive analysis of the nature of the environmental problems on various islands. These issues are also raised in: Ballegaard, Torben: Natur og turisme. Program til belysning af turismen og dens påvirkning af naturen på vadehavsøerne. Pilotprojekt Rømø, Miljøministeriet, Danmarks Miljøundersøgelser, September 1994; Bergh, J.C.J.M.: Tourism Development and the Natural Environment: a Model for the Northern Sporades Islands in Briassoulis, Helen and Jan van der Straaten: Tourism and the Environment. Regional, Economic and Policy Issues., Kluwer Academic Publishers, Dordrecht, 1992, pp 67-83; Camhis, M. and H. Coccossis: Environment and tourism in island regions in Planning and Administration, Vol 10, No 1 1983, pp 16-23; Wall, Geoffrey: International collaboration in the search for sustainable tourism in Bali, Indonesia in Journal of Sustainable tourism Vol 1, No 1, 1993, pp 38-47; and Wong, P.P (ed): Tourism vs environment: the case for coastal areas, Kluwer Academic Publishers, Dordrecht, 1993

The following sequence of inquiries into the conditions and consequences of tourism was undertaken for each of the islands:

- The type, continuation and future prospects of environmental problems related to the occurrence of tourism;

- Types of regulations instituted by authorities, and/or by other organizations and voluntary associations;

- The tourism industry's response to environmental regulations - or, conversely, its response to the lack of regulations;

- Business innovations carried out in reaction to environmental regulations .

This section provides a summary of the findings of the case studies reported on in the previous chapters[149]. A comparison is undertaken so as to further analyse the particular circumstances underlying a certain mode of environmental regulation. This comparison also attempts to highlight similarities and differences in the business sector's inclination to be innovative as a response to regulation.

The following key questions are asked in the course of this comparative research work:

- Can substantial differences or similarities be demonstrated in the environmental regulations, differences or similarities which might be explained by the types and seriousness of the environmental problems envisaged?

- Do the case studies demonstrate whether and how the same types of environmental obligations can be efficiently handled within different regulatory regimes?

- What kinds of innovations can be observed? Are some types of environmental regulation more efficient when it comes to stimulating innovations?

---

149   For details of the analysis consult chapters 2-4.

This study explores the relationship between tourism, environmental regulation and innovation, and it attempts to contribute explanations and guidelines for further investigation of the issue.

5.2. The three islands compared

To ensure an appropriate framework for comparisons, at least some of the features of the case study regions had to be identical. The most important common feature of Bornholm, Mallorca and the Isle of Wight is that their regional councils are politically elected, and that these councils control substantial elements of tourism development. In addition, they govern and supervise the implementation of important parts of the environmental policies.

Bornholm, Mallorca and the Isle of Wight all fulfil these criteria. Nevertheless, differences as well as similarities occur. Table 5.1. summarizes some crucial characteristics.

Table 5.1. Basic characteristics of case study regions

	Bornholm	Mallorca	Isle of Wight
Population	45,000	613,000	125,000
Area	590 sq. km	3,640 sq. km	330 sq. km
Tourism bednights	2.4 mil per year	50 mil per year	3.5 mil per year
Development of tourism since 1981	+ 14%	+ 98%	- 33%
Economic importance of tourism	5% of GDP	58% of GDP	20% of employment
Origins of tourists	German: 53% Danish: 30% Swedish: 14%	German: 35% British: 33% Spanish: 10%	British: 93%

It is of particular interest to note that Mallorca covers a geographical area that is considerably larger than the other case study regions, and that tourism is a sector of much greater importance to the Mallorcan economy than is the case with either of the other two regions.

Markets differ as well. The Isle of Wight is a destination which appeals predominantly to the domestic market, while Mallorca and Bornholm have significant inflows from Germany. German tourists tend to express a greater concern for the standard of the environment, a matter which should not be underestimated when analysing the efforts of the authorities and industries of the three islands to develop a more sustainable form of tourism.

The tourism growth rates are not comparable. The decrease of the tourist volume experienced on the Isle of Wight has caused investments to be retrenched, while the boom on Mallorca has allowed the island some latitude in economic terms (although more favourable economic conditions are not necessarily synonymous with the implementation of environmental investments).

The features shown in table 5.1. are not the only features assisting an understanding of the matter. Environmental constraints are not entirely identical in the three case study regions, as shown in the table below:

Table 5.2. Environmental constraints

	Bornholm	Mallorca	Isle of Wight
Changes in landscapes and towns	XX	XXX	X
Fresh water supply	XX	XXX	X
Waste water treatment	X	X	XXX
Noise	X	X	O
Solid waste treatment	XX	XX	XX
Energy supply and consumption	X	X	XX

XXX = Critical problem; XX = Problem of some importance; X = Problem of minor importance; O = Not regarded as a problem

Bornholm may be facing difficulties with its fresh water supplies, a matter of concern in relation to the development of tourism. Tourism is, however, a minor factor in regard to what/who is causing the problems, which are in fact predominantly caused by the use of fertilizers and pesticides in agriculture. On Bornholm, solid waste is efficiently

130

treated in a modern plant, but recycling has not been developed to any advanced stage. Energy savings, particularly in summer houses and hotels, could be enhanced, but Bornholm is already well ahead when it comes to institutional experiments and the implementation of renewable energy and public transport.

On Mallorca, the emphasis is on the drinking water supply. The ground water reserves are threatened, and dry summers require fresh water to be shipped in by tankers. Increasingly, the density of the built environment is regarded as an aesthetic and functional problem with a backlash effect on marketing, but this issue is only indirectly interrelated with the degradation of the environment. Waste water is being treated to meet EU standards, and discharges into the Mediterranean waters are limited to a minimum, as waste water is used for the irrigation of golf courses and in agriculture. Recycling programmes have been introduced, but land fills are still mainly used for solid waste.

On the Isle of Wight, environmental issues are primarily about solid waste and waste water treatment - areas where insufficient solutions have been found. In addition, tourism establishments are not really encouraged to reduce energy consumption and to limit waste. So far, the effect of tourism on landscapes and towns has been negligible - primarily as a consequence of the decline in the number of tourists visiting the island. Natural resources suited for the pursuit of "extreme sports" (hang-gliding, mountain-biking, angling, riding, climbing, etc.) are available and attractive on the Isle of Wight, and the growth of these special interest tourism markets may in future cause greater anxiety about erosion and landscape degradation than is presently the case. The Isle of Wight has a unique resource in its Victorian townscape and accommodation facilities, but lack of funding has led to neglect and necessitated some types of changes that neither comply with the atmosphere nor with modern environmental standards.

On the basis of this brief outline it can be seen that environmental discussions and actions on the three islands touch upon identical issues. But the situation is not equally serious on all islands, and the availability of natural resources and indigenous capacities to balance constraints varies enough to lead to differences in interpretation.

5.3. Agents and instruments of environmental regulation

The differences in the nature of the resources with which a destination was originally endowed in combination with the pressures tourism exerts on these assets are not necessarily and *per se* the sole motivators determining the choice of environmental policies and actions. Political priorities are often governed by other considerations than the seriousness of the situation.

In this section, the formal and informal agents in charge of environmental policy form the subject of a summarized comparative analysis.

Table 5.3. Agents of environmental regulation - dominant agents underlined

	Bornholm	Mallorca	Isle of Wight
Authorities	National government County council Municipalities	National government Regional government Municipalities	National government County Council
Private sector	The tourism industry Tour operators	The tourism industry The construction industry The tour operators	The tourism industry The privatised supply systems The tour operators
Voluntary sector	Environmental organizations	Environmental organizations	Environmental organizations (nature)

From table 5.3. it can be seen that the regulatory regimes of the three islands differ widely.

The regulation of the environment on Bornholm is predominantly the responsibility of the public authorities, and the system operates on the basis of a well-defined division of tasks. A framework planning and environmental control system constitutes the backbone of regulation, but there is still considerable scope for political influence on decisions at all levels. The municipalities and the county council are in charge of implementing national policies and priorities. Over the last few years, the county level has been increasing its influence on local environmental questions.

On Mallorca as well, the autonomous regional level is being strengthened, while the National Government only provides basic legislation. National legislation on the issue of sustainability in tourism is limited. In spite of the fact that the regional government has become considerably more influential in the course of the Spanish modernization process, the importance of business involvement in planning and politics should not be underestimated. In regard to environmental policies, foreign tour operators (representing the consumers) have recently started to make more heavy use of their bargaining power, not only when negotiating contracts with hotels, but also in their relations with local authorities. These unconventional co-operative relations between the authorities and the tour operators have turned out to be of crucial importance to the acceleration of the process leading towards more sustainable concepts of business and destination management.

One side effect of the deregulation and privatization policies and of relying more heavily on market forces has been that British regional governments have lost power over the last decade. As a result, a substantial amount of influence on environmental policies has been shifted away from immediate public dominance at the regional level and transferred into the hands of private contractors. On the Isle of Wight, the tourism industry has been too fragmented and impoverished to have gained any further leverage during the privatization and deregulation process. The environmental organizations (NGOs) that concern themselves with safeguarding English heritage, are powerful, however. Nowadays, these organizations tend - even more than some decades ago - to fill the vacuum left behind by the public authorities, who have withdrawn from the strong position they previously held in regard to planning and land ownership.

In Britain, private "self-regulatory" organizations, made up of tourism business members, fill other types of regulatory gaps, but such organizations have not yet come into play on the Isle of Wight.

Table 5.4. summarizes the most important groups of regulatory instruments directed towards the enhancement of tourism sustainability. In addition, the table reveals which instruments are given limited or no priority on each of the three islands.

Table 5.4. Environmental regulations predominantly in use

	Born-holm	Mal-lorca	Isle of Wight
Legislation and planning			
* Emission standards	XXX	XX	XX
* Compulsory use of specific technologies	XXX	0	0
* Zoning to control development	XXX	X	XXX
* Zoning to control access	X	0	X
Provision of infrastructure			
* Enhancing and maintaining natural resources	XXX	X	XX
* Trails, traffic infrastructure, etc.	XXX	X	XXX
* Interpretative infrastructure	XXX	0	XXX
* Strategic townscape improvements	XX	XXX	X
Green taxes, pricing policies			
* Entrance fees to natural resources	0	0	XX
* Levies, kurtax, etc.	0	0	0
* Licences	X	XX	X
* Energy tax, CO2 tax	XX	0	0
* Pricing policy, discharge tax on water	XX	0	0
* Developers pay costs	0	X	XX
Economic incentives			
* Loans, guarantees for sustainable investments	0	0	0
* Subsidies to compensate for aditional cost of sustainable solutions	XX	0	0
* Tax holidays	0	0	0
* Indirect subsidies through infrastructure	XX	X	0
Instruments based on business initiatives			
* Green audits	X	XXX	0
* Green awards and labelling	XX	XXX	0
* Demonstration projects	X	XX	0
* Proactive administration	X	XXX	0

XXX: Of major importance; XX: Of some importance; X: Of minor importance; O: Not on the agenda

To regulate the environmental impacts of tourism on *Bornholm*, a fairly large number of measures have been implemented. A typically Danish strategy is to diversify environmental policies. A strong emphasis is, however, still placed on "bureaucratic" measures such as legislation, planning and strategic provision of infrastructure.

Land-use planning is used to allocate areas for new development initiatives and creates frameworks determining the use of existing urban areas. County and municipal land use plans must be carefully co-ordinated with plans governing the provision of energy and water, with waste water treatment strategies, with development plans concerned with leisure facilities, and with nature protection and improvement plans.

Sector plans on energy, fresh water supply, waste water treatment, waste disposal, etc. fix fairly strict guidelines for activities of the public, semi-public or co-operative organizations in charge. To ensure financially feasible solutions, the use of specific types of energy supply systems (for instance district heating) is prescribed for consumers in certain areas.

Environmental standards are imposed on numerous specific operations. Most often, however, no particular emission standards are fixed for individual tourism enterprises. Where there are no standards or where standards cannot easily be fixed, proactive administration is used. Proactive administration is about consultations with the enterprises with the purpose of offering advice and discussing how, for instance, energy, water and waste savings can best be obtained.

As a supplement to the rules and bureaucratic regulations, the Danish government has introduced a set of green taxes (CO_2 taxes) to promote energy savings and create revenues. In the future, these taxes are expected to influence tourism enterprises quite heavily. There is some possibility of applying for subsidies from the tax revenue funds for investments in energy saving equipment.

The third dominant instrument used on Bornholm concerns interpretation. In particular, the Bornholm County Council has involved itself in efforts to regulate tourist behaviour. Pamphlets suggest tours, trails are provided, guided tours and visitor centres are made available. Often voluntary organizations co-operate with the Council in providing these measures and facilities.

Individual hotels and the hotel association of the island have received the introduction of a (national) green label very positively, and an approval procedure has been initiated at a number of hotels.

These past few years, the regional government of *Mallorca* has been reinforcing its planning capacities, partly as a response to EU legislation and other opportunities provided by the EU. The need to intensify planning activities and to fix higher standards has increased, along with the expansion of tourism and the necessity of fighting the gradual degradation of the tourist resorts. The tourists' negative response to degradation is anticipated to be even more pronounced in the future if adequate action is not taken.

But still, the implementation of regulatory instruments depends heavily on a continuous process of negotiation with the tourism industry and with other sectors related to tourism, for instance the construction sector. The decision to initiate the POOT plan, which will eventually regulate the future supply of hotel capacity (size and quality), has been in the pipeline for a long time, and its implementation still depends on the active co-operation of the industry.

Green taxes have not been introduced on Mallorca, and investment subsidies and other types of financial incentives have only infrequently been offered to the tourism industry. The provision of interpretative measures is almost always left to the commercial sector or to voluntary organizations, and the level of activities is low. Green labelling of hotels and resorts is in preparation, and this issue receives considerable attention from business associations and particularly from tour operators, who are much in favour of such measures.

Although it has been given fairly low priority over the last few years, planning on the *Isle of Wight* is still important, and land-use regulation relating to tourism is crucial.

In order to increase efficiency, the British government decided to simplify planning procedures, deregulate where possible and to privatize the water and energy sypply services, etc. Taxpayers were supposed to benefit from tax cuts. Consumers of water, waste treatment, energy, etc. would be given a freer choice of suppliers. The overall standards would be in the hands of government agencies, but operational details could be decided by contractors.

The objectives of sustainable tourism on the one hand and of the contracting enterprises needing to make a profit on the other hand might coincide and pull in the same direction. But on the Isle of Wight these mechanisms have not in most cases operated in accordance with the above vision. The free market forces seemed to favour rather short-sighted solutions, e.g. within the field of waste water treatment. Recycling programmes, which previously formed part of the public waste handling system, have been abandoned as they were not strictly profitable. Privatized suppliers have no particular motive for encouraging their private and business customers to save water and energy, and no campaigns to this effect have been established on the Isle of Wight.

The voluntary sector (such as the National Trust) plays a "gap-filling" role in regulation. The voluntary sector does, however, still have to operate on commercial terms. Instead of paying for the maintenance of heritage landscapes and interpretative facilities via their taxes, consumers are asked to pay via membership of NGOs, donations and entrance fees. NGO fundraising in the business sector is becoming very common. For instance, the waste water treatment company operating on the Isle of Wight supports local environmental groups[150].

---

150   Princen, T: NGOs: Creating a niche in environmental diplomacy in Princen, T. and Mathias
         Finger (eds): Environmental NGOs in world politics, Routledge, London, 1994, pp 29-47

Public access to protected areas relies on a very strong inclination and tradition among the British population for making the most of the learning and leisure experiences available in the countryside. Land designations and access schemes are commonplace, and the Isle of Wight is no exception.

To conclude: environmental regulation of tourism on the three islands is based on very different traditions and ideologies. Figure 5.1. shows a "regulatory triangle" within which regulation can take place. The philosophy underlying the figure is that regulation of the behaviour and the interaction between actors will always be necessary where these actors compete for the right to use the same resources. Regulation may, however, take place in various ways and in various combinations.

The upper corner of the triangle represents the "bureaucratic model", where legislation, planning, emission standards, etc. make up the most essential elements of regulation. The left corner depicts the "clan model", where groups and associations of businesses are powerful enough to ensure that the group members will stick to certain high ethics and standards. The third corner represents the "market model", which is based on the assumption that consumers' demands will, if necessary, change the behaviour of the industry. In recognition of the fact that market forces are not always sufficient to ensure the implementation of environmental standards, one might apply financial instruments such as subsidies, green taxes, levies, etc. in order to influence market mechanisms.

The Danish model is predominantly a bureaucratic model. In Spain, dominant business powers tend to lead to the introduction of instruments which require businesses and their organizations to co-operate closely with the political system. The British set-up tends to let the market forces play a major role, but planning is still regarded as a viable instrument.

Figure 5.1. Three regimes of environmental policy

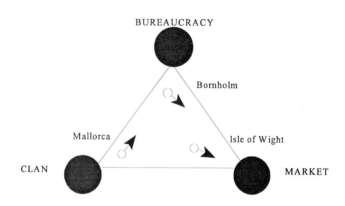

These regimes of regulation are not stable. Over the past decade, all three islands have gradually moved some way out of their corner in the triangle - a matter which is indicated by the gradual change in the composition of the instruments played in the environmental policy orchestra.

For instance, the Danish Government introduced green taxes on energy consumption to alleviate the pressure on constrained resources. These taxes should be seen as an instrument with a dual purpose, viz. to create revenues and to motivate savings. The movement towards the market corner of the triangle has been quite obvious, although government influence is still considerable and selective.

The Danish model does not involve the same degree of privatization as for instance the British model, where consumers are supposed to be selecting the more sustainable suppliers via their purchasing behaviour. On the Isle of Wight doubt has been expressed as to whether environmental issues are high on consumers' priority lists - suppliers at least do not seem to think so. The official environmental agencies have a "backstop function", setting up statutory standards, granting and monitoring consents, and taking legal action, if required.

British environmental policy has not ceased moving towards the "market" corner. On the Isle of Wight, the quest for continued privatization and deregulation has tended to result in the abandonment of programmes and initiatives belonging to the other regimes in the triangle.

The Mallorcan case is interesting in the sense that the regional government has increased its power, and uses its influence to put greater emphasis on planning and back statutory standards. To ensure future competitiveness on the price and image-sensitive charter markets, there is a strong inclination to meet EU environmental standards. Although actively promoting higher environmental standards, the business community is not able to accelerate this development on its own, and so co-operation with a demanding authority is needed.

5.4. Innovations resulting from environmental protection

In the above section, it was shown that regulatory regimes are not stable, but can be influenced by new inputs from markets, by changes in the seriousness of the environmental situation, or by changes in the political climate.

Business practice is not a matter of perfect stability, either. Businesses tend to switch products, production processes, management styles, distribution channels, etc. when more profitable solutions offer themselves. Innovations are often aggregates of many small changes. But more comprehensive developments could be, ideally, the outcome of a massive green wave in tourism.

Has environmental regulation already brought about changes in business practice, changes which might be classified as innovations? Do these innovations represent a step forward in the competitiveness of the enterprises and the destinations?

The three case study regions can on no account be considered highly innovative. Numerous empty gaps in table 5.5. indicate that action has been piecemeal, and that no comprehensive response to environmental challenges has as yet taken place.

Table 5.5. Innovative actions as a response to regulation

	Bornholm	Mallorca	Isle of Wight
Product innova-tions			Commodification of the nature product
Process innova-tions	Fast diffusion of energy and water saving technologies		
Management innovations			
Innovations of logistics		Tour operators as environmental inter-mediaries	
Institutional innovations		Institutionalization of auditing procedures + auxiliary organizations	

Does this lack of response indicate that regulation is an inefficient instrument when it comes to motivating the business sector to come up with innovations? Or is the specific regulatory instrument that was introduced on a particular island much too weak to make enterprises and organizations move any further than is absolutely necessary to ensure "business as usual"?

Product innovations are improvements or changes in services or products that are perceived by someone (consumers, producers, competitors) as new. A product innovation does not necessarily require a change in the physical product. It is enough if marketing parameters or complementary services lead some observers to believe that the product actually is different.

The British tradition of commodifying the natural environment is of long standing, but in recent years the strategy has been given new dimensions. For instance, on the Isle of Wight new events are being organized involving other types of sports than before. These events utilize the natural environment to promote commercial purposes. The nature product is being continuously developed. In addition, establishments are remodelling the educational product according to new demands and based on new technical opportunities. For instance, multimedia auxiliary tools have been developed. This market niche can be promoted not only because of a carefully regulated and protected countryside, but just as much as a response to another type of regulation, namely the National Curriculum.

The influence of voluntary organizations on protection work has increased, and the creation of alliances with large commercial enterprises with the purpose of raising funds has contributed to making NGOs more powerful. The commercialization of the nature product - the use of entrance fees, sales from well-furnished shops, guided tours, etc. also matches the objective of regulation through the market. Tourists take what they find is "value-for-money" - a much used marketing idiom in Britain.

None of the other case study regions cultivated the perfection of the nature product to such a degree as the Isle of Wight. However, it could be maintained that tourists' access to the natural resource, for instance, in the shape of well-maintained bicycle trails on Bornholm is just as innovative. But these trails are also considered one of the range of services provided for the residents by the state, not simply a resource destined for commercial exploitation.

Process innovations raise the performance of operations already in the portfolio. Productivity gains are the self-evident objective of most enterprises, including tourism businesses. Investments in technology will often be made to replace or increase the efficiency of operations when costs suddenly or gradually rise. Process and product innovations may go hand in hand.

Green taxes on water, waste water, energy and solid waste treatment have efficiently promoted investments in the Bornholm tourism industry. Managers are perfectly able to comprehend that investments will lead to savings in the volumes consumed so that higher prices can (partly) be compensated for. Government subsidies are available to tourism industries to enable them to undertake environmental audits and to carry out feasibility studies prior to investments. In this way taxes combined with subsidies have aided a speedy implementation of new practices in tourism on Bornholm.

Businesses devoting themselves to technical efficiency can be awarded a green label. The marketing activities undertaken by the national labelling organization render the environmental practice of a company visible to its customers. Thus, the product will present itself as different or changed: a "green" hotel, a "responsible" attraction.

Managerial innovations are carried out to increase job satisfaction and/or productivity. No substantial managerial innovations have been observed on the three islands, at least not any which could be linked environmental regulation. Minor initiatives such as staff training are found, but the educational systems have not succeeded in embedding the issue firmly into the curricula.

Innovations of logistics embrace creative reorganization of the flow of goods, people (tourists) and information. The Mallorca case is interesting when it comes to the flow of information.

Tourism to Mallorca is dominated by package holidays, where tour operators occupy an important role as intermediaries. Over the last few years, German tour operators in particular have emphasized the need to further develop the flows of environmental information to and from customers. Specially established environmental departments within German tour operators constitute new market intelligence systems which ensure a continuous flow of environmentally relevant information to and from Mallorca.

Information on the attitudes of customers and their requirements, for instance, is channelled to hoteliers and destinations, stimulating their environmental awareness. This tends to accelerate investments and other actions catering for the environment. Conversely, customers are requested to help alleviate particular constraints, for instance by saving water.

Institutional innovations. As part of the European Environmental Audit Scheme, Mallorca established a new co-ordinating organization to undertake all auditing activities. This organization is in many ways similar to the German Grüner Koffer label and the Danish Grøn Nøgle label. However, in co-operation with the tourism industry, the regional government of Mallorca decided to place more far-reaching obligations in the hands of the organization ECOTUR. A particularly innovative measure was the establishment of a Geographical Information System (GIS) which is to be employed both in land-use planning and the environmental auditing of destinations.

The potential scope of environmentally based innovations is much wider than suggested by the measures adopted and implemented by the three case study islands[151]. Why are they so reluctant in this respect? Why do they not contribute more actively to a changed concept of tourism?

Table 5.6. summarises some very important barriers to innovation.

---

151   For a systematic review of innovations in sustainable tourism, see Hjalager, Anne-Mette: Innovations in sustainable tourism - an analytical typology, unpublished conference paper, 1995

Table 5.6. Main barriers to innovation

	Bornholm	Mallorca	Isle of Wight
Economic composition of industry	Ownership of facilities fragmented (summer houses). Lack of consensus		Ownership of facilities fragmented (hotels). Associations lack consensus
Customer demand	Lack of organized consumer pressure		Lack of organized consumer pressure
Financial incentives		No green taxes, no investment subsidies available to the private sector	No green taxes, no investment subsidies available to the private sector
Legislation and planning			Political climate favouring deregulation
Environmental pressure groups	Exist, but lack influence	Exist, but lack influence	

A fragmented industrial structure is an important reason explaining the lack of an organized response to environmental problems and constraints, particularly on Bornholm and the Isle of Wight. On Bornholm, the summer houses - a major tourist resource - are owned by individual families. On the Isle of Wight, the proprietors of small hotels and guest houses are frequently retired couples who are not particularly inclined to increase size, quality and professionalism. Agreement among tourism enterprises to engage in a proactive response cannot be obtained, as individual enterprises tend to focus on competing among themselves. Regulations are regarded as costly external nuisances, not stimuli for innovation.

Tourism to Mallorca is highly organized. The absolute majority of the tourists arrive on package tours. On behalf of their customers, the tour operators possess an immense bargaining power, a power which is to an increasing extent used to stimulate environmental awareness at the destination. Bornholm and the Isle of Wight cater predominantly for individual tourists, although the package tour market has recently increased. However, consumer pressure is still diffuse and therefore individual tourism enterprises do not find it easy to grasp. The ferry companies are major organizers of packaged tours, but they have only just started to inquire into environmental issues, and they do not regard themselves as exponents of consumer pressure in this respect.

Spanish and British environmental regulations only include green taxes and investment incentives at a very insignificant level. Such measures are regarded as distorters of competition and are therefore considered unwarranted. It is interesting to note that the costs of the supply services on Mallorca and the Isle of Wight are comparable to (or even more expensive than) those paid on Bornholm, and yet the industries on Mallorca and the Isle of Wight have only implemented marginal saving measures. It might be concluded that the implementation of green taxes creates a "panic" which provokes action. Races to obtain government investment subsidies have always been considered a favourite sport on Bornholm, but neither the Isle of Wight nor Mallorca have ever been provided with similar incentives designed to promote technological developments.

In Britain, deregulation is a hot topic on the political agenda and in consequence on the Isle of Wight. In its purest version, deregulation is not agree compatible the maintenance or upgrading of the environment. The tendency to weaken responsibility in this direction is, however, partly counterbalanced by the existence of voluntary organizations and environmental pressure groups on the Isle of Wight. In the two other regions studied, the opposite type of balance is more prominent. Mallorca even favours strengthening the planning and legislative instruments.

The hypothesis put forward in this section was that regulation spurs innovative activities. This hypothesis cannot easily be tested, as regulation is only one of many factors that lead to change in businesses and at destinations. Comparing the three regions does, however, yield new insights into the composition of environmental regulation measures and their effects.

5.5. Discussion

Individual companies and consumers will attempt to externalize the environmental impact of their activities to zones where they are not themselves affected. If the space for discharges is unlimited, emissions might go on. But this is not the case, and the social costs[152] from pressure on the environment tend to rise. This study shows that the long-term social costs to be paid by future generations are recognized especially on Mallorca, increasingly also on Bornholm, but not very much on the Isle of Wight.

In principle, business inefficiencies created by externalization can be eliminated if private negotiations between all concerned parties can be arranged. It is commonly assumed, however, that the costs of ensuring the dissemination of appropriate information to all parties would turn private negotiations between polluters and pollution victims into an infeasible solution to the environmental problems with which they are concerned.

---

152   Coarse, Ronald: The problem of social cost in Journal of Law and Economics, Vol 3, 1960, pp 1-44

As was shown in this study, there are now millions of tourists, and the tourism industry is fragmented into many small independent suppliers. It is impossible for all the people involved to acquire relevant information, and it is even less possible to identify the relevant partners for negotiation. The transaction costs (costs of deciding, planning, arranging, and negotiating the actions to be taken and of settling on the terms of exchange; costs of changing plans, renegotiating terms, and resolving disputes as changing circumstances may require; and costs of ensuring that parties perform as agreed[153]) are simply much too high.

This is where the tasks of regulation are taken over by specialized organizations of varied composition.

We have been considering three ways of organizing tourist destinations: Bornholm is a predominantly "bureaucracy" governed regime, Mallorca could be characterized as a "clan" dominated regulatory model, and the Isle of Wight is approaching the "market perfection" corner of the model presented in Figure 5.5.

According to Ouchi[154], in a *bureaucratic* relationship each party contributes resources (levies, tax funds, etc.) to the corporate body which mediates the relationship by placing a value on each contribution and then compensating it fairly. "The perception of equity in this case depends upon a social agreement that the bureaucratic hierarchy has the legitimate authority to provide this mediation." (p 130).

Typically, bureaucracy will emphasize technical expertise and the ability to handle the ever increasing volumes of information on the environment professionally. The strengthening of the regional level to the disregard of the municipalities on Bornholm could be seen as a way of coping with a higher degree of complexity. Contrary to occasional protests, and in spite of continual attempts to negotiate decisions with the bureaucracy, the business sector does not seriously challenge the system. There is a high degree of acceptance of the beneficial effects planning has on the tourism industry. Companies and the population have gradually come to accept the idea of selective green taxing.

---

153   Milgram, Paul and John Roberts: Bargaining costs, influence costs, and the organization of
        economic activity in James, E. Alf and Kenneth A. Shepsle (eds): Perspectives on positive
        political economy, Cambridge University Press, New York 1990, pp 57-89

154   Ouchi, William G.: Markets, Bureaucracies and Clans in Adminstrative Science Quarterly,
        Vol 25, March 1980, pp 129-141

This could be seen as an expression of the fact that bureaucracies are efficient when goal incongruence is fairly high - the need to make immediate financial profits and the need to secure adequate resources for future generations represent incompatible motives. At the same time, performance ambiguity is high - regulation has to pay regard to many agents, and uncertainty about the actual and future impacts of the methods used is considerable. Mediation and conscious change of action is required.

In connection with the case studies reported on here, it is interesting to observe that the Mallorcan regulatory regime is moving increasingly towards the bureaucratic model and away from the *clan* model. Ouchi noted that clans are particularly efficient when there is a high congruence of goals. A high congruence of goals has existed for many years. The population, the tourism industry, the tour operators, the construction industry and the authorities shared the objective of growth in tourism. To achieve the objective, a rather simplified set of measures was employed. The Mallorcans were primarily concerned with building new hotels, while the tour operators were in charge of marketing.

Environmental constraints increased the necessity to establish controlling organizations. It is no longer considered unimportant how the island develops, and many other voices are being raised advocating further protection beyond the immediate objectives that the business representatives would regard as feasible.

Mallorca is, however, not entirely adopting the bureaucracy model. Tour operators and business associations are still very powerful, and they influence the direction of the regulations that the authorities intend to implement and enforce.

According to Ouchi the *market model* is efficient when goal incongruence is high, but not when performance ambiguity is low.

On the Isle of Wight, there is no unified sense of the direction future developments on the island should take. The preservation of landscape is an issue, partly in conflict with the wish to develop tourism, which again is in opposition to the retired population who want the island to remain a quiet place. Other types of environmental issues are raised infrequently but always balanced against such issues as tax cuts and the lowest possible prices on supply and other services. Accordingly, the Isle of Wight expresses, in many respects, incongruent goals.

The British government's and the local authorities' response to these conflicting goals is reflected in the attempt to implement the market model with the fewest possible modifications. Performance is regulated through price, a very unambiguous instrument. In other words, it is believed that if money rules, the objectives of regulation will be efficiently achieved with the least possible interference. Successful implementation will allow a substantial deregulation of former bureaucracies.

The Isle of Wight is a passable illustration of the fact that the market is a practical mediator as long as certain conditions are fulfilled. Within the framework of this philosophy, such a thing as for instance disposing of waste water in the British channel is perfectly acceptable, and this practice will not be changed until someone confronts the polluter with a claim for compensation on the grounds that he/she has suffered a loss of economic opportunities.

Voluntary nature protection organizations operate through the acquisition of land and through the commercialization of the nature product - which also complies very well with the market model. They do, however, only involve themselves in limited segments of the environmental problem leaving out such items as energy provision and waste water disposal.

It is interesting to note that the UK is the home of "self-regulation". Organizations are established to promote and monitor voluntary environmental actions of the business sector. The idea is that the absence of environmental ethics - expressed by means of plans and legislation - will delay development towards sustainability. To the above organizations it is, however, more important that, in due course lack of public regulation might increase the risk of future emergency interventions, which might prove economically devastating to the industry. Part of the logic of self-regulating organizations is that enterprises should always be ahead of future public regulatory issues so as to gain advantages through proactive behaviour. Accordingly, self-regulating organizations will tend to compensate for any lack of sufficient regulation - but mostly they operate within the logic of the market system. [155] The World Travel and Tourism Environmental Research Centre collects and disseminates information on best practice to member companies. A Green Globe is awarded to initiatives with wide-ranging perspectives. The members of these organizations are predominantly large airlines, hotel chains, car rentals, tour operators, etc. None of these are represented on the Isle of Wight.

To conclude, the three case study regions illustrate the scope of three dominant regimes of regulation. The case study method seems the best way of reaching a more holistic understanding of the situation and the prospects of sustainability on the islands.

It has been shown that environmental regulation may be efficiently achieved in all types

---

155   Elkington, John: Responsibility for sustainability in Envrionment and Development, WTTERC Newsletter no 4, 1994, p 6; and Jenner, Paul and Christine Smith: The tourism industry and the environment, EUI special report no 2453, London, February 1992

of regimes, and that there is some interchangeability between measures and room for a combination of policies with elements from two or all of the regimes. A lack of efficiency experienced within one regime generates interest in adopting elements from other regimes in order to combine them with or replace previous measures. The Danish movement towards green taxes, and the Mallorcan adoption of the bureaucratic planning model are examples of this combination and interchangeability of activities.

It is equally interesting to note that the private sector's inclination to innovate largely matches its dominance in the regulatory regime. Regulation does have an impact on innovation, and the type of regulation chosen determines where and how development takes place. New or changed products, the composition of production processes, the logistics of flows and the creation of institutions are stimulated by regulation. Even when there is a lack of regulation or when public authorities consciously attempt to deregulate and reinstate market forces, innovations are not entirely excluded. Yet it can be seen from the case studies that the Isle of Wight, where regulation is most "laissez-faire" and dominated by market measures, has an "apathetic" private sector which mostly ignores environmental issues altogether.

It should be acknowledged that regulation is not the only stimulator of innovation[156], and this makes the identification of the connections difficult. For instance, on Mallorca market demand is an agent of change, whereas stable and unresponsive markets on Bornholm tend to lead to more passive attitudes. The attitude of tourists visiting the Isle of Wight, who regard environmental problems as being of minor or no importance, does, of course, contribute to an explanation for the lack of innovative efforts.

5.6. Perspectives for future research

Far more than was originally anticipated, these case studies of this book end up telling the story of impaired memory and selective repressions. The research deals with the lack of inclination to consider comprehensive and proactive approaches to sustainable tourism on the three islands selected. Piecemeal strategies were, however, identified. Innovative initiatives are reported. The minds of the tourist businesses and the authorities are not entirely closed to environmental matters, but the issue is typically not placed at the top of the agenda.

To the researcher, the optimum point of departure is to be allowed to study phenomena which form part of firmly established behaviour. In this way, it is possible to provide

---

156   Magat, Wesley A: The effects of environmental regulation on innovation in Law and
         Contemporary Problems Vol 43, 1979, pp 4-25

an explanatory framework for causes, processes and consequences. Compared to this ideal situation, the task of having to explain how and why certain events do *not* take place is far more complicated, and the consequences of this non-action could lead to pointless speculation - unless the emphasis is placed on analysis of the barriers to developing sustainable tourism.

This research into non-action or limited actions could have resulted in methodological difficulties and risks. At the same time it was, however, a considerable and important challenge to identify why events do not occur, why enterprises and authorities do not change their behaviour. Economic research does, for instance, attempt to find explanations that will answer the question of why enterprises, local areas or nations settle on what is already given them, thus sub-optimizing in relation to their opportunities[157]. Knowing about resistance to change is essential to policy development, making it possible either to devise measures to change existing behaviour, or alternatively to enhance the exploitation of the advantages that in some respects derive from being behind.

Accordingly, it has not been without merit to analyse the lack of proactive behaviour, and the case studies attempted to learn from and supplement the rich research tradition.

This research study has attempted to widen the perspectives of the future studies that will be undertaken within the field of tourism and the environment. The study emphasizes the need to investigate more carefully the mechanisms leading towards or away from sustainability. Primarily, this study looked into the character and role of regulation. But other driving forces pulling towards or away from sustainable tourism also need more in-depth research. For instance, the change in consumer attitudes, an issue which is - strangely enough - still largely uncharted and where no particular emphasis has been placed in transnational comparative studies.

Another set of driving forces is found in the role played by the suppliers of the tourism industry. The supply side has many facets, including the labour market, technology supplies, the financial markets, etc. The regulatory issues raised in this report would benefit from the balancing effect achievable via the inclusion of these groups of driving forces.

Three island regions were selected for case studies, and the choice finally made served the purpose of the study well. However, other types of destinations, e.g. urban areas or

---

157   Elster, Jon: Explaining technical change. Studies in rationality and social change. Cambridge University Press, Cambridge, 1983 and Winter, Sidney G.: Optimization and evolution in the theory of the firm in Day, Richard H. and Theodore Grove: Adaptive Economic models, Academic Press, New York, 1975 pp 73-118

inland locations, face other problems and prospects. Systematic analyses of comparable and different destinations are needed to enhance the explanatory value of these case studies.

Environmental processes are dynamic in nature, and policy programmes are meant to maintain or restore some presumed "equilibrium" with nature. This will of course be a continuous process of small and large adjustments. However, beyond this process of continuous development lies a dynamic of social learning, of which we have no comprehensive understanding. Parson and Clark illustrate the need to focus on the learning processes not only of individuals, but also of groups, formal organizations, professional communities, or entire societies[158]. The key point is that learning takes place in social settings or is socially conditioned.

Therefore, longitudinal studies in a comparative framework of sustainable tourism development processes will afford an opportunity of enhancing the preliminary findings of this study and add to it a deeper understanding of real-world dynamics.

---

158   Parson, Edward A. and William Clark: Sustainable development and social learning. Theoretical perspectives and challenges for design of a research programme in Gunderson, Lance H. et al (eds): Barriers and bridges to the renewal of ecosystems and institutions, Columbia University Press, New York, 1995, pp 428-460

List of references

Adams, W.M.: Places for Nature: Protected Areas in British Nature Conservation in Goldsmith, F.B and Warren A.(eds): Conservation in Progress, Wiley and Sons, Chichester, 1995

Ajuntament de Calvià: First operation of Calvià's desaturation plan, n.d.

Ajuntament d'Alcúdia: Satzung des Ausschusses für die Förderung und Bewilligung der Ökotouristischen Plaketten, n.d.; and TUI: Urlaub und Umwelt Mallorca, n.d.

Alvarez, Antonio Garcia: Environmental impact assessment, Spain in European Environmental Yearbook, 1990

Ashdown Environmental Limited.: Water supply and sewage disposal specialist study, 1993, refered to by IFTO: Planning for sustainable tourism. The ECOMOST project, n.d.

Ballegaard, Torben: Natur og turisme. Program til belysning af turismen og dens på-virkning af naturen på vadehavsøerne. Pilotprojekt Rømø, Miljøministeriet, Danmarks Miljøundersøgelser, September 1994;

Beller, W., P. d'Ayala and P. Hein (eds): Sustainable development and environmental management of small islands, Man and Biosphere Series, UNESCO, 1990

Bergh, J.C.J.M.: Tourism Development and the Natural environment: a model for the Northern Sporades Islands in Briassoulis, Helen and Jan van der Straaten: Tourism and the Environment. Regional, Economic and Policy Issues, Kluwer Academic Publishers, Dordrecht, 1992

Blasco, Avelino: Legislacion Turistica de Baleares, supplement to the ECOMOST project

Boehmer-Christiansen, Sonja and Jim Skea: Acid politics: Environmental and energy policies in Britain and Germany, Belhaven Press, London and New York, 1991

Boers, H. and M. Bosch: The earth as a holiday resort. An introduction to tourism and the environment, Utrecht, 1994

Bornholms Amt: Energy and Environment, 1992

Bornholms Amt: Friluftslivets interesseområder, Rønne, 1984

Bornholms Amt: Interreg Bornholm, 1992

Bornholms Amt: Regionplan, 1993, Rønne, 1994

Bornholms Amt: Spildevand 1994, 1995

Bornholms Amt: Tillæg til regionplan 1985 om skovrejsning, December 1991

Bornholms Amt: Vandmiljøet på Bornholm, Resultater af 5 års overvågning, n.d.

Bornholms Amt: Vandplan Bornholm

Bramsnæs, Annelise and Erik Bølling-Ladegaard: Miljøvurdering. Implementering af VVM i Danmark, Kunstakademiets Arkitektskole, April 1992

Briassoulis, Helen and Jan van der Straaten: Tourism and the environment: An overview in Briassoulis, Helen and Jan van der Straaten: Tourism and the Environment. Regional, Economic and Policy Issues, Kluwer Academic Publishers, Dordrecht, 1992

Camhis, M. and H. Coccossis: Environment and tourism in island regions in Planning and Administration, Vol 10, No 1, 1983

Central Statistical Office: Regional trends, 1995 edition, London, 1995

Cherry, Gordon E.: Changing social attitudes towards leisure and the countryside in Britain, 1890-1990 in Glyptis, Sue (ed): Leisure and the environment, Belhaven, London 1993

Clark, Gordon et al: Leisure Landscapes. Leisure, Culture and the English Countryside: Challenges and Conflicts, CSEC, Lancaster University, 1994

Coarse, Ronald: The problem of social cost in Journal of Law and Economics, Vol 3, 1960

Coll Perello, Margarita: Turismo y medio ambiente: Hacia un turismo compatible, student dissertation, Universitat de las Islas Baleares, n.d.

Collier, Ute: Energy and Environment in the European Union. The challenge of integration, Avebury, Aldershot, 1994

Commission of the European Communities: Towards Sustainability. A European Community Programme of Policy and Action in Relation to the Environment and Sustainable Development, 1992

Conrad, Jobst: Nitrate pollution and politics. Great Britain, the Federal Republic of Germany and the Netherlands, Avebury, Aldershot, 1990

Croall, Jonathan: Preserve or destroy. Tourism and the environment, Gulbenkian Foundation, London 1995

Dandata

David Bruce: Walled Towns, n.d.

David Bruce: A Handbook of Good Practice for Sustainable Tourism in Walled Towns, Bristol Business School, October 1993

Department of the Environment: Planning policy guidance: Tourism, PPG 21, November 1992

Dowling, Ross: An environmentally-based planning model for regional tourism development in Journal of Sustainable Tourism, Vol 1, No 1, 1993

Eadington, William and Valene L. Smith: The emerging of alternative forms of tourism in Smith, Valene L. and William R. Eadington (eds): Tourism alternatives. Potentials and problems in the development of tourism, University of Pensylvania Press, Philadelphia, 1992

Eagles, Paul F.J., Per Nilsen, Manao Kachi and Susan D. Buse: Ecotourism: an annotated bibliography for planners & managers, The Ecotourism Society, North Bennington, Vermont, 1995

Eber, Shirley (ed): Beyond the Green Horizon. Principles for Sustainable Tourism, WWF, UK, Godalming, 1992

Elkington, John: The green capitalists, Victor Gollancz, UK, 1989

Elkington, John: Responsibility for sustainability in Envrionment and Development, WTTERC Newsletter no 4, 1994

Elster, Jon: Explaining technical change. Studies in rationality and social change.

Cambridge University Press, Cambridge, 1983

English Tourist Board: Isle of Wight Tourism Study, September 1981

English Tourist Board: Tourism and the environment. Maintaining the balance, London 1991

Environment Committee: The environmental impact of leisure activities, House of Commons, London, 1995

European Union, Regulation no. 1836/93 allowing voluntary participation by companies in the industrial sector in a Community eco-management and audit scheme, OJ.C 168/1, CEC, Luxembourg, 1993

Farrell, Bryan H. and Dean Runyan: Ecology and Tourism in Annals of Tourism Research, Vol 18, No 1 1991

Federation of Nature and National Parks in Europe: Loving them to death, Grafeanu, 1993

Finansministeriet: Grønne afgifter og erhvervene, København 1994

Framke, Wolfgang: Turismens belastning af miljøet in Turisme nr 8, 1993

Friends of the Earth, Mednet: Sustainable tourism in the Mediterranean, n.d.

Gittins, John: Community involvement in environment and recreation in Glyptis, Sue (ed): Leisure and the environment, Belhaven, London, 1993

Glasson, John et al: Introduction to environmental impact assessment, UCL Press, London, 1994

Govern Balear: DOT Islas Baleares. Hacia un Desarrollo Sostenible del Territorio, n.d.

Govern Balear: Gesetz über Naturlandschaften gemäss städtebaulichen Regelungen für besonders geschützte Zonen der Balearen, pamphlet

Govern Balear: La despesa turística, 1993

Govern Balear: The Balearic Innovative Region, 1992

Govern Balear: Pla Estratègic de Competitivitat de las Islas Baleares, Tom 1: Diagnòstic, 1994

Govern Balear: Pla Estratègic de Competitivitat de las Islas Baleares, Tom 2, Propostes, 1994

Gunn, Clare A.: Environmental Design and Land Use in Ritchie, J.R. Brent and Charles R. Goeldner (eds.): Travel, Tourism and Hospitality Research: A Handbook for Managers and Researchers, New York, 1987

Haig, Nigel: EEC. Policy and implementation in European Environmental Handbook, 1991, pp 86-87

Handler, Thomas: Regulating the European Environment, Chancery Law Publishing 1994

Hasløv and Kjærsgaard: Notat vedr. spørgeskemaundersøgelsen 1994, February 1995

Heaton, Andrew: Conservation and the National Rivers Authority in Goldsmith, F.B. and A. Warren (eds): Conservation in progress, Wiley and Sons, Chichester, 1995

Hiranyakit, Somchai: Tourism Planning and the Environment in UNEP Industry and Environment, Jan-Mar 1984

Hjalager, Anne-Mette: Tourism and the environment - the innovation connection in Journal of Sustainable Tourism, forthcoming

Hjalager, Anne-Mette: Dynamic innovation in the tourism industry in Cooper, C.P. and A. Lockwood (eds): Progress in Tourism, Recreation and Hospitality Management, Vol 6, John Wiley & Sons, Chichester, 1994

Hjalager, Anne-Mette: Innovations in sustainable tourism - an analytical typology, unpublished conference paper, 1995

Hjalager, Anne-Mette: Innovation patterns in sustainable tourism - an analytical typology in Tourism Management, Vol 18, No 1, 1997

Holm-Petersen, Erik, Anne-Mette Hjalager, Wolfgang Framke and Peter Plougmann: Turisme/fritid - en erhvervsøkonomisk analyse, Erhvervsfremme Styrelsen, København, 1993

Hopfenbeck, Waldemar and Peter Zimmer: Umweltsorientiertes Tourismusmanagement. Strategien, Checklisten, Fallstudien, Verlag Moderne Industrie, Landsberg/Lech, 1993

HORECON: Afrapportering af forprojekt: "Bornholm - en ø med miljøbevidst turisme", 1995.

HORECON: Bornholm. En ø med miljøvenlig turisme, n.d.

IBATUR: Espais Naturals de les Illes Balear, 1992

IDAE(Instituto para la Diversificacion y Ahorro de la Energia): Guía de las Energías Renovables en Baleares/4, 1995

IFTO: Planning for sustainable tourism. The Ecomost project, Lewes, UK, n.d.

IFTO: Planning for sustainable development, The Ecomost Project, n.d.

Inskeep, Edward: Tourism planning. An integrated and sustainable development approach, Van Nostrand Reinhold, NY, 1991

Isle of Wight AONB Joint Advisory Committee: Isle of Wight AONB Management Plan Summary, August 1994

Isle of Wight Council: Unitary development plan, Consultation draft, February 1996

Isle of Wight County Council: Coastal path leaflets

Isle of Wight County Council: Electricity for the Island. A County Council Initiative, leaflet, n.d.

Isle of Wight Tourism and Southern Tourist Board: Isle of Wight tourism strategy, April 1994

Iwand, Michael (TUI): Instruments, procedures and experiences of integrating the environment into tourism development by a major tour operator, paper at the World Conference on Sustainable Tourism, Lanzarote, April 1995

Jenner, Paul and Christine Smith: The tourism industry and the environment, EUI special report no 2453, London, February 1992

Jensen, Susanne et al: Borntek. Evaluering af et program for erhvervsudvikling på

Bornholm 1988-1992. Institut for grænseregionsforskning, Åbenrå, 1994

Jensen, Susanne: Turismens økonomiske betydning i Danmark i 1991, Institut for grænseregionsforskning, Åbenrå, 1993

Jørgensen, Kaj, Nielsen I. Meyer and Henning Pilegaard: Energiplan for en grøn ø, Borgen, 1986

Lanquer, Robert: Tourisme et environnement en Méditerranée. Enjeux et prospective, Economica, Paris, 1995

Ley 8/1987, de 1 de abril, de Ordenación Territorial de las Islas Baleares

Ley de los espacios naturales, metioned in Govern Balear: Gesetz über Natur-landschaften gemäss städtebaulichen Regelungen für besonders geschützte Zonen der Balearen, pamphlet

Lindberg, Kreg and Hawkins, Donald E. (eds): Ecotourism. A guide for planners and managers, The Ecotourism Society, North Bennington, Vermont, 1993

Lov nr 9 af 1. marts 1992 om Naturbeskyttelse

Lov nr 590 af 27.6.1994 om Miljøbeskyttelse

Lovbekendtgørelse nr 383 af 14.6.1993 om Planlægning

Lovforslag L 209 af 6.4.1995 om ændring af lov om kuldioxid af visse energiprodukter.

Lovforslag L 210 om ændring af lov om energiafgift af mineralolieprodukter m.v. og lov om afgift af stenkul, brunkul og koks, og lov om afgift af elektricitet,

Lovforslag L 213 af 6.4.1995 om afgift af svovl

Magat, Wesley A: The effects of environmental regulation on innovation in Law and Contemporary Problems Vol 43, 1979

Masterton, Ann M.: Environmental ethics in Harssel, Jan van: Tourism. An exploration. Prentice Hall, Englewood Cliffs, 1994

Mathieson Alister and Geoffrey Wall: Tourism. Economic, Physical and Social Impacts, Longman, Harlow, 1982

McIntyre, George: Sustainable tourism development: guide for local planners, WTO, Madrid, 1993

Merriam, Sharan: Fallstudien som forskningsmetod, Studentlitteratur, Lund, 1994

Milgram, Paul and John Roberts: Bargaining costs, influence costs, and the organization of economic activity in James, E. Alf and Kenneth A. Shepsle (eds): Perspectives on positive political economy, Cambridge University Press, New York 1990

Miljø- og Energiministeriets bekendtgørelse nr. 847 af 30. september 1994 om supplerende regler i medfør af Lov om Planlægning

Miljø- og Energiministeriet: Vejledning om planlægning i kystområderne, København 1995

Miljøministeriet: Naturforvaltning, Årsberetninger and Amtsrådsforeningen: Amterne i naturen, København, 1994

Miljøministeriet: Miljøtilstanden i Danmark, København 1991

Miljøministeriets cirkulære af 19. december 1991: Cirkulære om planlægning og administration af kystområder; now included in: Lovbekendtgørelse af 16. august 1994 om planlægning

Ministerio de Comercio y Turismo: Situacion actual del turismo en las Islas Balear, n.d.

Moe, Mogens: Miljøret - Miljøbeskyttelse, Gad, København, 1994

MSS Marketing Research: Isle of Wight pre and post omnibus study 1994/95

Munch-Petersen, Nils Finn: The Bornholm vacation product, research paper, Bornholms Forskningscenter, March 1996

Nexø kommune: Delrapport om projekt KURS, 21 July1994

Nexø kommune: Miljøhåndbog for turistvirksomheder i Nexø kommune, n.d.

OECD: The Impact of Tourism on the Environment, General Report, Paris, 1980

Ouchi, William G.: Markets, bureaucracies and clans in Administrative Science Quarterly, Vol 25, March 1980,

PA Consultants: Isle of Wight visitor survey, May 1994

Parson, Edward A. and William Clark: Sustainable development and social learning. Theoretical perspectives and challenges for design of a research programme in Gunderson, Lance H. et al (eds): Barriers and bridges to the renewal of ecosystems and institutions, Columbia University Press, New York, 1995

Pearce, Douglas: Tourism and environmental research. A review in International Journal of Environmental Studies, Vol 25, 1985

Pigram, John J.: Environmental Implications of Tourism Development in Annals of Tourism Research, Vol VII, No 4 1980

Pombo, Fernando: Spain in Brealey, Mark (ed): Environmental Liabilities and Regulation in Europe, International Business Publishing Limited, The Hague, 1992

Poon, Auliana: Tourism, technology and competitive strategies, CAB International, Wallingford, 1993

Princen, T: NGOs: Creating a niche in environmental diplomacy in Princen, T. and Mathias Finger (eds): Environmental NGOs in world politics, Routledge, London, 1994

Rafn, Thomas: Turismens økonomiske betydning for Bornholm, Bornholms Forsknings-center, 1995

Rafn, Thomas: Turismens betydning for de danske amter, Bornholms Forskningscenter, Nexø, 1996

Rambøll, Hannemann and Højlund: Tourist project no 9. Environmental analysis of summer houses/holiday houses, Esbjerg, July 1994

Ravenscroft, Neil: The environmental impact of recreation and tourism development: A review in European Environment, Vol 2, part 2, 1992

Robledo, Marco Antonio and Julio Batle: Integral tourism re-planning in a mature destination: Mallorca's POOT, unpublished paper, n.d.

Rådets Forordning (EØF) nr 1836/1993 af 29.6.1993 om industrivirksomheders frivillige deltagelse i fællesskabsforordning for miljøstyring og miljørevision

Samvirkende Bornholmske Turistforeninger and Bornholms Amt: På tur i Bornholms natur, 1989

Schertler, Walter: Eco-management in tourism in Steinchke, Albert (ed): Umwelt-orientiertes Management im Tourismus, Europäisches Tourismus Institut an der Universität Trier, 1994

Schønemann, Steen: En ø uden tilskud. En analyse af betalingerne mellem Bornholm og det øvrige Danmark og et bud på, hvad der sker, hvis den ophører, Bornholms Forskningscenter, 1995

Selstad, Tor: Det nordiske reiselivet i Europa, Oppland Distriktshøgskole, September 1992

Sidaway, Roger and Han van der Voet: Getting on Speaking terms: resolving conflicts between recreation and nature in coastal zone areas of the Netherlands. A literature study and case study analysis, Landbouwuniversiteit Wageningen, September 1993; and

Simonsen, Peter Saabye and Birgitte Jørgensen: Cykelturisme. Økonomisk og miljømæssig bæredygtighed?, Bornholms Forskningscenter, 1996

Southern Water Services: Conservation and the environment. The Report for 1994/1995

Southern Tourist Board, Visitor Research Service: Isle of Wight Strategy Research 1994, May 1994

Symes, Tom and Victoria Phillips: England and Wales in Beadley, Mark (ed): Environmental liabilities and regulation in Europe, International Business Publishing, The Hague, 1992

Tarrio, Filipe Ruza: Organizational structure, Spain in European Environmental Yearbook, 1990

Tarrio, Filipe Ruza: Sea/Coast, Spain in European Environmental Handbook, 1990

The 4 Towns Project - 1993. Analisis Cuestionario Residentes Alcudia

The World Bank and The European Investment Bank: The Environmental Program for the Mediterranean. Preserving a Shared Heritage and Managing a Common Resource, Luxembourg, 1990

Therivel, Riki et al: Strategic environmental assessment, Earthscan Publications, London, 1992

UK Government: Sustainable development: the UK Strategy, HMSO, 1994

UK Government: Sustainable development. The UK strategy, HMSO, London, 1994

Unpublished data from the tourist survey 3rd quarter 1995, Bornholms Forskningscenter

Wall, Geoffrey: International collaboration in the search for sustainable tourism in Bali, Indonesia in Journal of Sustainable tourism Vol 1, no 1, 1993

Wight, P.: Enviromentally responsible marketing of tourism in Cater, Erlet og Gwen Lowman: Ecotourism. A sustainable option? Wiley, Chichester, 1994

Wight, P: The greening of the hospitality industry: economic and environmental good sense in Seaton, A.V. (ed): Tourism. The state of the art. John Wiley & Sons, Chichester 1994

Winter, Sidney G.: Optimization and evolution in the theory of the firm in Day, Richard H. and Theodore Grove: Adaptive Economic models, Academic Press, New York, 1975

Wong, P.P (ed): Tourism vs environment: the case for coastal areas, Kluwer Academic Publishers, Dordrecht, 1993

WTTERC: Travel and tourism. Environment and development, World Tourism & Travel Review, 1993

Yin, Robert K.: Case study research. Design and methods, Applied Social Research Methods Series, Vol. 5, Sage Publications, Newbury Park, 1989

Ziffer, Karen: Ecotourism: An Uneasy Alliance, Conservation International and Ernst & Young, Fall 1989